365 DAYS OF KETOGENIC DIET RECIPES

NEW PROOFREAD VERSION 2017

EMMA KATIE

Check out more books by Emma Katie at:
www.amazon.com/author/emmakatie

CONTENTS

Breakfast recipes

Lunch and Dinner recipes

Keto Snacks

Sweet snacks

Salty snacks

Ketogenic Burgers - Lunch and Dinner Bonus Recipes

Keto Slow cooker recipes

Pressure Keto recipes

Ice creams...as desserts

Other Desserts...

INTRODUCTION

Dear reader,

What is the Keto diet you are probably wondering? Keto or ketogenic diet is a type of diet that restricts the intake of carbohydrates and promotes higher intake of fats. Although this may sound odd and contrary to all you have heard, carbs are our enemy and because of them we usually get that not so cute belly. Additionally, latest scientific studies have shown that Keto diets help with weight loss but also keeps the blood sugar on right track, because fats have no effect in blood sugar and insulin levels.

Many carbohydrates occur naturally in plant-based food, like grains. Your body uses carbohydrates as its main fuel source. Sugars and starches – carbohydrates, are broken into simple sugars, during digestion process. When broken, these molecules are absorbed in blood stream, these molecules are known as glucose or blood sugar.

Rising levels of glucose trigger body to release insulin, which helps glucose to enter into blood cells. Some glucose, in our body is used for energy, fueling all your activities, from running to simple breathing. All unused glucose is stored in liver, muscles and other cells for later use. If glucose is not used it is turning into fat.

The idea behind the low-carb diet is a reduction of carbohydrates which turn into glucose and potentially in body fat. If carbohydrate levels are lower, insulin will decrease and therefore your body will be forced to burn the stored fat for energy which results in a slimmer figure.

Breakfast recipes

CASHEW AND BERRIES CREAM

Preparation time: 15 minutes   Servings: 2

Ingredients:

½ cups raw cashews, soaked in water for 3 hours
¼ teaspoon vanilla paste
1 lemon, juiced
2 tablespoons water

1 cup raspberries
½ cup strawberries, pureed or mashed with fork
½ teaspoon cinnamon

Directions:

In a food processor pulse the cashews, vanilla paste, lemon juice and water.
Process until smooth. Divide the mix between the bowls. Top with raspberries and pureed strawberries.
Sprinkle with cinnamon before serving.

Nutritional Info: Per serving

Calories: 171
Total fat: 12.3g

Cholesterol: 0mg
Total Carbs: 12.9g

Protein: 5.8g

OMELET WITH CHEESE

Preparation time: 5 minutes   Cooking time: 5 minutes   Servings: 2

Ingredients:

4oz. goats cheese, crumbled
6 eggs, whisked lightly
2 tablespoons parsley, fresh, chopped

2 tablespoons butter
Salt and pepper – to taste

Directions:

Whisk eggs with parsley in a bowl, season with salt and pepper to taste.
Melt the butter in a non-stick skillet over medium-high heat, until it starts to bubble.
Add eggs and cook for 4 minutes, sprinkle the eggs with crumbled cheese.
Fold the eggs in half and continue cooking for 1 minute, then serve.

Nutritional Info: Per serving

Calories: 469.8
Total fat: 37.9g

Cholesterol: 615.2mg
Total carbs: 1.7g

Protein: 29.5g

HARD BOILED EGGS WITH MASCARPONE

Preparation time: 5 minutes   Cooking time: 7 minutes   Servings: 4

Ingredients:

4 eggs, whole
2 tablespoons butter, room temperature
2 tablespoons Mascarpone cheese

1 tablespoon chives, fresh and chopped
Salt and pepper – fresh ground, to taste

Directions:

Cook eggs in pot of simmering water for 7 minutes, remove from the heat and leave in warm water for 5 more minutes. Place eggs in cold water and rinse quickly under cold water and peel
Chop the rinsed eggs and divide between two bowls.
Add chives, mascarpone and butter and stir well to combine. Season with salt and pepper before serving.

Nutritional Info: Per serving

Calories: 151.3   Cholesterol: 211.5mg   Protein: 6.4g
Total fat: 13.6g   Total carbs: 0.4g

DEVILED EGGS WITH CREAMY FILLING

Preparation time: 5 minutes   Cooking time: 10 minutes   Servings: 6

Ingredients:

6 large eggs
1 tablespoon melted butter
2 garlic cloves
¼ cup mayonnaise

¼ teaspoon Dijon mustard
1 jalapeno pepper, seeded and minced
Salt and white pepper – to taste

Directions:

Cook the eggs for 10 minutes in simmering water over medium-high heat, remove from the heat and set aside for 3 minutes. Pour hot water out and add cold, let the eggs rest for 8 minutes.
Peel the eggs and cut in half, lengthwise, remove the egg yolks and place in a bowl.
Break up the egg yolks with a fork and stir in melted butter, white onion, mayonnaise, mustard, and jalapeno and season to taste with salt and pepper.
Arrange the egg white shells onto plate and fill with prepared egg yolk mixture, using a spoon or piing bag.
Cover and refrigerate until ready to serve.

Nutritional Info: Per serving

Calories: 129   Cholesterol: 190mg   Protein: 6.5g
Total fat: 10.2g   Total Carbs: 3.2g

SAVORY CHEDDAR WAFFLES

Preparation time: 5 minutes   Cooking time: 10 minutes   Servings: 4

Ingredients:

3 eggs, whole
3oz. cream cheese
1oz. sharp Cheddar cheese, grated
2 tablespoons coconut flour

1 teaspoon baking powder
1 jalapeno, seeded and minced
1 pinch cumin, ground
Salt and pepper – to taste

Directions:

Combine eggs, cream cheese, coconut flour, baking powder and cumin in food blender; blend until smooth.
Once the ingredients are smooth add cheddar and jalapeno; process until blended thoroughly.
Preheat waffle iron and pour over prepared waffle mix, cover and cook for 5-6 minutes.
Top with salsa or avocado before serving.

Nutritional Info: Per serving

Calories: 151
Total fat: 13.1g

Cholesterol: 150mg
Total Carbs: 1.5g

Protein: 7.5g

BREAKFAST SAGE PATTIES

Preparation time: 5 minutes   Cooking time: 8 minutes   Servings: 8 patties

Ingredients:

1lb. ground pork
2 tablespoons powdered Erythritol
1 teaspoon pure maple extract
1 teaspoon salt

2 tablespoons fresh sage, chopped or 2 teaspoons dried
2 garlic cloves, minced
¼ teaspoon black pepper

Directions:

In a bowl, combine all the ingredients.
Shape the mixture into 8 patties. Press each patty with oiled hands to 1-inch thick.
Heat large skillet over medium-high heat. Add some oil.
Cook the patties for 4 minutes per side.
Serve while still hot.

Nutritional Info: Per serving/patty

Calories: 82
Total fat: 2.0g

Cholesterol: 41mg
Total Carbs: 0.3g

Protein: 14.9g

Coconut-flax Waffles

Preparation time: 5 minutes   Cooking time: 4 minutes   Servings: 4

Ingredients:

8 whole eggs
½ tablespoon Ceylon cinnamon, ground
2 tablespoons coconut milk or whole milk
½ teaspoon nutmeg, ground

½ cup flax flour
½ teaspoon baking soda
2 tablespoons melted butter

Directions:

Place all ingredients in a food blender.
Pulse until blended thoroughly and place aside to rest for 5 minutes.
Meanwhile, preheat the waffle iron to medium-high heat. Drop batter in center of waffle iron and cook for 3-4 minutes.
Serve while still hot.

Nutritional Info: Per serving

Calories: 225   Cholesterol: 243mg   Protein: 12.8g
Total fat: 18.9g   Total Carbs: 3.2g

Cream Cheese Waffles

Preparation time: 5 minutes   Cooking time: 5 minutes   Servings: 4

Ingredients:

4oz. cream cheese
4 eggs, whole
½ teaspoon Ceylon cinnamon, ground

1 pinch nutmeg
Some butter and sugar free syrup – to serve with

Directions:

Place all ingredients in food blender and pulse until blended thoroughly.
Place the batter aside to rest for few minutes and meanwhile, preheat the waffle iron.
Pour the batter over waffle iron to cover ¾ of the surface and cook waffles for 4-5 minutes.
Serve while still hot, with butter and sugar-free syrup.

Nutritional Info: Per serving

Calories: 162   Cholesterol: 195mg   Protein: 7.7g
Total fat: 14.3g   Total Carbs: 1.1g

ALL SPICE WAFFLES

Preparation time: 5 minutes   Cooking time: 10 minutes   Servings: 4

Ingredients:

12 tablespoons almond flour
2 teaspoons allspice
1 teaspoon vanilla extract
½ teaspoon baking soda
4 eggs, whole

2 tablespoons Erythritol
4 tablespoons cream cheese
1 teaspoon orange zest
2 tablespoon heavy cream

Directions:

Mix together almond flour with allspice and baking in a bowl.
Combine together eggs with Erythritol and fold into flour mixture.
Preheat waffle iron and pour the batter onto waffle iron. Cook for 3-4 minutes.
Meanwhile combine cream cheese, orange zest, and heavy cream to make the filing.
Cut waffles into quarters and spread cream cheese evenly over half of the waffles, top with remaining waffles, to create a sandwich and serve.

Nutritional Info: Per serving

Calories: 170
Total fat: 14.2g

Cholesterol: 185mg
Total Carbs: 3.3g

Protein: 8.0g

KETO OMELET WRAP

Preparation time: 5 minutes   Cooking time: 5 minutes   Servings: 1

Ingredients:

3 eggs, whole
1.5oz. salmon, smoked, sliced
1 spring onion, medium, chopped
1 tablespoon butter

¼ avocado, sliced
2 tablespoons cream cheese
2 tablespoons chives, fresh and chopped
Salt and pepper – to taste

Directions:

Beat eggs with salt and pepper in a bowl.
Combine chives and cream cheese in separate bowl.
Melt butter in medium-size skillet over medium-high heat, add the whisked eggs and cook for 30 seconds until edges are set, pull the edges gently so runny eggs slide to bottom of pan. Continue cooking for 1-2 minutes until you get a kind a tortilla.
Transfer the omelet onto a plate and spread over cream cheese; top with salmon, avocado and spring onion; wrap and serve.

Nutritional Info: Per serving

Calories: 423
Total fat: 34.3

Cholesterol: 462mg
Total Carbs: 2.9g

Protein: 27.0g

BLUEBERRY WRAPS

Preparation time: 5 minutes   Cooking time: 5 minutes   Servings: 2

Ingredients:

4 eggs, whole
4oz. cream cheese
2/3 cup blueberries
2 tablespoons Erythritol

3 tablespoons whipped cream, sugar-free
Some additional blueberries
½ teaspoon vanilla extract

Directions:

Blend the cream cheese, vanilla, blueberries, and sweetener in a food blender.

Heat non-stick skillet over medium-high heat and grease slightly with some butter; pour 1/3 cup of batter into skillet and cook for 2 minutes, flip carefully and cook for 1 minute more.

Spread whipped cream over tortillas and sprinkle with blueberries; wrap and serve.

Nutritional Info: Per serving

Calories: 420   Cholesterol: 215mg   Protein: 16.0g
Total fat: 35.6g   Total Carbs: 6.5g

ZUCCHINI MUFFINS

Preparation time: 5 minutes   Cooking time: 30 minutes   Servings: 12 muffins

Ingredients:

1 ½ cups flax flour
1 ½ cups zucchini, shredded and squeezed
3 eggs, whisked lightly
1/3 cup almond milk
¾ cup feta, crumbled
1 tablespoon chives, chopped

1 teaspoon basil, dried, crushed
¼ teaspoon salt
2 teaspoons baking powder
2 tablespoons coconut flour
¼ teaspoon onion powder
3 tablespoons butter, melted

Directions:

In a large bowl whisk together the almond flour, salt, coconut flour, basil, onion powder, garlic powder and baking powder.

In a separate bowl whisk the eggs with milk and until blended. Fold liquid ingredients in flour mixture and add chives, followed by feta cheese; stir until combined. Stir in zucchinis.

Line 12-hole muffin tin with paper cases and fill with prepared mixture to 2/3 full.

Bake the muffins in preheated oven for 30 minutes at 325F or until firm to the touch. Place on wire rack to cool slightly before removing from muffin tin and serving.

Nutritional Info: Per serving/muffin

Calories: 85   Cholesterol: 57mg   Protein: 3.1g
Total fat: 7.6g   Total Carbs: 1.7g

SWEET EGG PORRIDGE

Preparation time: 5 minutes   Cooking time: 5 minutes   Servings: 1

Ingredients:

2 eggs
¼ cup heavy cream
2 tablespoons butter

Sweetener, to taste
1 pinch Ceylon cinnamon

Directions:

Whisk the eggs, cream, and sweetener, to taste in a bowl.
Melt the butter in small saucepan. Add the eggs and immediately reduce the heat to low.
Cook the eggs until eggs curdle and have grain like structure, like the porridge, stirring constantly.
Remove from the heat and transfer in a bowl. Sprinkle with cinnamon.

Nutritional Info: Per serving

Calories: 433   Cholesterol: 330mg   Protein: 11.9g
Total fat: 42.9g   Total Carbs: 1.5g

RASPBERRY MUFFINS

Preparation time: 5 minutes   Cooking time: 20 minutes   Servings: 6 muffins

Ingredients:

½ cup raspberries, fresh
3 eggs, whole and room temperature
1/3 cup coconut flour
½ teaspoon vanilla
15 drops Stevia

¼ cup butter, melted
1 pinch salt
3-4 tablespoons water
½ teaspoon baking powder

Directions:

Preheat oven to 375F and line 6-hole muffin tin with paper cases.
Whisk eggs until well blended; add butter, whisking to blend thoroughly.
Add salt, Stevia and vanilla and continue mixing; mix in baking soda, coconut flour and mix until almost combined.
Add raspberries and mix gently to incorporate in prepared batter; spoon the mixture into paper cases and bake for 18 minutes.
Place on wire rack to cool slightly before serving.

Nutritional Info: Per serving/muffin

Calories: 106   Cholesterol: 102mg   Protein: 3.0g
Total fat: 9.9g   Total Carbs: 1.6g

LMOND-PEANUT MUFFINS

Preparation time: 5 minutes　　　Cooking time: 25 minutes　　　Servings: 12 muffins

Ingredients:

6 whole eggs
1 teaspoon cinnamon
¼ cup peanut butter, organic
2/3 cup almond flour
2 tablespoons coconut oil
1 pinch salt

10 drops Stevia
¼ teaspoon nutmeg
1 tablespoon butter
¼ cup heavy cream
¼ cup crushed and toasted almonds
2 tablespoons Erythritol

Directions:

Preheat oven to 350F and line 12-hole muffin tin with paper cases.

Combine together almond flour, cinnamon, nutmeg, salt and Erythritol in a bowl.

Combine butter, peanut butter and coconut oil in microwave safe bowl; microwave for 30 seconds; stir well and pour over almond flour mix.

Stir in the eggs, Stevia and heavy cream and mix well. Spoon the batter into paper cases, sprinkle with crushed almonds and bake for 20-25 minutes; place on wire rack to cool slightly before serving.

Nutritional Info: Per serving/muffin

Calories: 114　　　Cholesterol: 88mg　　　Protein: 4.7g
Total fat: 10.2g　　　Total Carbs: 2.0g

EGG AND BACON BITES

Preparation time: 10 minutes + inactive time　　Servings: 4

Ingredients:

¼ cup butter, room temperature
4 slices bacon, cooked and crumbled
2 tablespoons mayonnaise

1 pinch chili powder
2 eggs, whole, large
Fresh ground salt and pepper – to taste

Directions:

Boil the eggs for 10 minutes (if large) and remove from the heat. Transfer the eggs into bowl filled with cold water and when chilled peel. Rinse quickly under cold water and slice.

Cut the softened butter into a bowl and add sliced eggs.

Mash all with a fork and add mayonnaise, chili powder and season to taste with salt and pepper.

Cover with plastic wrap and refrigerate for 30 minutes. Meanwhile, crumble the bacon and place into shallow dish. Form balls from the egg mixture and roll into crumbled bacon. Refrigerate for 10 minutes more before serving.

Nutritional Info: Per serving

Calories: 265　　　Cholesterol: 135mg　　　Protein: 10.0g
Total fat: 24.1g　　　Total Carbs: 2.2g

PUMPKIN PANCAKES

Preparation time: 12 minutes   Cooking time: 10 minutes   Servings: 4

Ingredients:

2oz. almond flour
2oz. flax meal
1 cup heavy cream
2 eggs
1oz. egg white protein

1 teaspoon vanilla extract
4 drops stevia
1 teaspoon baking powder
1 pinch salt
½ cup pumpkin puree

Directions:

Place all ingredients in a food blender.
Blend until smooth.
Place the batter aside to rest for 10 minutes. If you feel it is too dry add ¼ cup water or coconut milk.
Heat 1 teaspoon of coconut oil in a skillet. Pour a ladle of batter onto oil and cook for 2-3 minutes per side.
Transfer onto a plate and serve.

Nutritional Info: Per serving

Calories: 198   Cholesterol: 82mg   Protein: 16.7g
Total fat: 17.3g   Total Carbs: 7.7g

BANANA YOGURT

Preparation time: 5 minutes   Cooking time: 30 minutes   Servings: 4

Ingredients:

1 cup almond milk
½ pcs banana, sliced
1 pinch cinnamon

2 tablespoons cashews, soaked in water for
20 minutes, drained
2 tablespoons chia seeds

Directions:

Place all ingredients in a food blender.
Process until smooth.
Allow to rest for few minutes and serve after.

Nutritional Info: Per serving

Calories: 151   Cholesterol: 0mg   Protein: 1.5g
Total fat: 14.4g   Total Carbs: 6.7g

CHOPPED ZUCCHINIS BOWL

Preparation time: 5 minutes   Cooking time: 5 minutes   Servings: 4

Ingredients:

2 cups zucchinis, grated

1 tablespoon coconut flour

1 cup almond milk
3 egg whites
2 tablespoons cocoa powder, raw

3 drops stevia
1 pinch cinnamon
2 tablespoons raspberries, fresh

Directions:

In a food blender combine the almond milk and zucchinis. Pulse until blended thoroughly.
Heat the mixture in sauce pan over medium-high heat. Add the egg whites and bring mixture to boil.
Cook, stirring until thickened, for 2 minutes. Add in the coconut flour, stevia, cinnamon and cocoa powder.
Continue cooking until you have mixture similar to porridge, for 2 minutes more.
Remove from the heat and top with fresh raspberries.

Nutritional Info: Per serving

Calories: 168
Total fat: 14.8g

Cholesterol: 0mg
Total Carbs: 7.4g

Protein: 5.3g

BACON AND EGGS

Preparation time: 5 minutes

Cooking time: 30 minutes

Servings: 6

Ingredients:

6 hardboiled eggs
3.5oz. cream cheese

12 slices bacon, organic
¼ teaspoon thyme, dried

Directions:

Preheat oven to 400F and line baking sheet with parchment paper.
Combine the cream cheese and thyme in a bowl.
Cut the eggs in half, lengthwise and remove the egg yolk.
Fill the egg whites with cream cheese and wrap each egg half with 1 piece of bacon. Arrange onto baking sheet and bake for 30 minutes. Remove from the oven and serve with egg yolks on side.

Nutritional Info: Per serving

Calories: 326
Total fat: 26.0g

Cholesterol: 224mg
Total Carbs: 1.4g

Protein: 20.9g

TURKEY-APPLE PATTIES

Preparation time: 5 minutes

Cooking time: 10 minutes

Servings: 4

Ingredients:

8oz. ground turkey breast
½ cup apple, shredded
½ teaspoon sage, dried
¼ cup almonds, chopped

¼ teaspoon black pepper, ground
1 pinch salt
1 pinch paprika

Directions:

In a large bowl combine the ground turkey, shredded apple, sage, almonds and spices. Mix with wooden spoon until combined. Form ½-inch thick patties.

Heat some oil in large skillet over medium-high heat; add prepared patties and cook for 4 minutes per side. Serve while still hot.

Nutritional Info: Per serving/patty

Calories: 157

Cholesterol: 42mg

Protein: 17.7g

Total fat: 7.2g

Total Carbs: 4.3g

BREAKFAST EGG SALAD

Preparation time: 5 minutes

Cooking time: 10 minutes

Servings: 4

Ingredients:

6 eggs, whole

1 teaspoon lemon juice

1 teaspoon mustard, Dijon style

2 tablespoon mayonnaise

1 pinch salt

Directions:

Place the eggs in sauce pan and cover with cold water.

Bring to boil and boil for 10 minutes. Remove from the heat and drain the hot water; pour over the cold water and place aside until the eggs are cool enough to handle.

Peel the eggs place in food processor; pulse until chopped.

Add the remaining ingredients and stir well. You can either serve the salad at room temperature or chill before serving.

Nutritional Info: Per serving

Calories: 127

Cholesterol: 247mg

Protein: 8.6g

Total fat: 9.3g

Total Carbs: 2.6g

EGGS IN THE CLOUDS

Preparation time: 5 minutes

Cooking time: 10 minutes

Servings: 6

Ingredients:

4 eggs

¼ cup bacon, crumbled

¼ cup grated cheese, like Pecorino Romano

¼ cup chives, chopped

Salt and pepper, to taste

Directions:

Separate the eggs; place the egg whites in a bowl and whisk with pinch of salt until stiff peaks form.

Fold in the chives, bacon and grated cheese. Preheat oven to 400F and line baking tray with parchment paper.

Drop the egg whites onto baking sheet. Making four mounds and make a deep well in the center. Place the egg yolk in center of each mound and bake for 3-5 minutes or until the eggs are set.

Season with salt and pepper before serving.

Nutritional Info: Per serving

Calories: 145

Cholesterol: 130mg

Protein: 10.8g

Total fat: 10.9g

Total Carbs: 0.6g

CARDAMOM PANCAKES

Preparation time: 5 minutes   Cooking time: 10 minutes   Servings: 6

Ingredients:

2 eggs
2 tablespoons mashed banana
4 cardamom pods, ground
3 tablespoons coconut milk
1 ½ tablespoons coconut flour

1/4teaspon baking soda
½ teaspoon vanilla paste
½ teaspoon apple cider vinegar
1 tablespoon ghee or butter

Directions:

In a food blender combine the flour, cardamom and baking soda; pulse few times to blend.
Add the mashed banana, coconut milk, eggs and vanilla paste. Pulse until blended thoroughly.
Heat the ghee in large skillet over medium heat; add large tablespoon of batter per pancake and cook for 1 ½ minutes. Carefully flip the pancake and cook for 30 seconds more. Repeat with remaining batter and serve immediately, while still hot.

Nutritional Info: Per serving

Calories: 70   Cholesterol: 60mg   Protein: 2.5g
Total fat: 5.7g   Total Carbs: 2.6g

CHIA BOWL WITH FRUITS

Preparation time: 5 minutes   Servings: 4

Ingredients:

1 teaspoon vanilla paste
1 tablespoon Erythritol
2 cups coconut or almond milk

¼ cup chia seeds, whole
1 kiwi, sliced
2 tablespoons almonds, crushed

Directions:

In a bowl combine the chia seeds with milk. Place aside for 1 hour.
After the time has run, add the vanilla paste and Erythritol. Divide the chia seeds mix between the serving bowls and top with sliced kiwi and crushed almonds.

Nutritional Info: Per serving

Calories: 305   Cholesterol: 0mg   Protein: 3.6g
Total fat: 30.2g   Total Carbs: 9.1g

CHOCOLATE-HAZELNUT WAFFLES

Preparation time: 5 minutes   Cooking time: 10 minutes   Servings: 12

Ingredients:

6 cups hazelnut meal (simply place
hazelnuts in food blender and process)

2 tablespoons cocoa powder
3 tablespoons hazelnut or walnut oil

2 tablespoons coconut flour
1/3 cup almond milk
3 tablespoons erythritol

4 eggs
¼ teaspoon stevia

Directions:

Preheat waffle iron.

In a large bowl combine the hazelnut meal, cocoa powder, coconut flour and erythritol.

In a separate bowl whisk the hazelnut oil with milk, eggs and stevia.

Fold milk mixture into flour mixture and stir until you have thoroughly blended mix.

Grease the waffle iron with some oil and spread ¼ cup of batter per pancake over the waffle iron.

Close the waffle iron and cook until crispy and brown. Remove and repeat with remaining batter. Serve after.

Nutritional Info: Per serving

Calories: 383
Total fat: 36.7g

Cholesterol: 55mg
Total Carbs: 10.1g

Protein: 9.1g

PUMPKIN BAGELS

Preparation time: 5 minutes   Cooking time: 25 minutes   Servings: 8

Ingredients:

3 eggs, whisked
1/3 cup coconut flour
3 tablespoons flax meal
1 ½ teaspoon pumpkin spice
¼ cup almond milk
2 tablespoons coconut oil, melted
½ cup pumpkin puree, organic and pure

1 teaspoon vanilla paste
1 pinch salt
15 drops stevia
1 tablespoon erythritol
½ teaspoon baking soda (combined with 1 teaspoon apple cider)

Directions:

Preheat oven to 350F and grease 8-hole donut or bagel pan.

In a large bowl sift the coconut flour. Add the flax seeds, pumpkin spice and salt.

In separate bowl whisk the eggs, milk, stevia, vanilla paste, erythritol, pumpkin puree and coconut oil. Fold the milk mixture into flour mix and stir until well combined.

Spoon the batter into prepared pan and bake for 23-25 minutes. Remove and place on the wire rack to cool slightly before removing.

Serve with cream cheese.

Nutritional Info: Per serving

Calories: 95
Total fat: 8.1g

Cholesterol: 61mg
Total Carbs: 3.8g

Protein: 3.2g

SNICKERDOODLE CREPES

Preparation time: 5 minutes   Cooking time: 10 minutes   Servings: 4

Ingredients:

8oz. cream cheese, room temperature
6 eggs
1 teaspoon cinnamon

1 tablespoon erythritol
1 cup raspberries, fresh

Directions:

Mash the raspberries and combine with 3oz. cream cheese. Place aside.

In a blender combine the remaining cream cheese, eggs, cinnamon and erythritol.
Pulse until blended through.

Heat the large non-stick skillet over medium-high heat. Pour enough batter to form 6-inch pancake. Cook for 2 minutes, flip and cook for 30 seconds more.

Once the pancakes are prepared spread the raspberries mix over the pancakes and roll each pancake. Serve immediately.

Nutritional Info: Per serving

Calories: 310
Total fat: 26.5g

Cholesterol: 208mg
Total Carbs: 5.2g

Protein: 13.0g

AVOCADO-VANILLA CREAMY SMOOTHIE

Preparation time: 5 minutes   Servings: 4

Ingredients:

½ avocado, peeled, stoned
2 tablespoons almond butter
1 cup almond milk

1 cup half-and-half
10 drops stevia
1 tablespoon chia seeds

Directions:

In a food blender combine all ingredients by order.
Pulse until blended thoroughly. Allow to rest for 5 minutes before serving.

Nutritional Info: Per serving

Calories: 317
Total fat: 30.7g

Cholesterol: 22mg
Total Carbs: 8.6g

Protein: 5.3g

LEMON-BLUEBERRY MUFFINS

Preparation time: 5 minutes   Cooking time: 30 minutes   Servings: 8

Ingredients:

5 tablespoon coconut flour, sifted
1/3 cup erythritol

1 ½ teaspoons lemon zest, grated finely
¼ cup heavy cream

3 eggs

½ cup blueberries, fresh

Directions:

Preheat oven to 350F and line 8-hole muffin tin with paper cases.

In a bowl whisk the erythritol, eggs and heavy cream until well mixed.

Add the coconut flour and whisk until smooth. Let stand for 5 minutes before adding lemon zest and fresh blueberries. Stir very gently and spoon the batter between paper cases.

Bake the blueberries for 25-30 minutes or until inserted toothpick comes out clean.

Serve after at room temperature.

Nutritional Info: Per serving

Calories: 49

Cholesterol: 67mg

Protein: 2.5g

Total fat: 3.3g

Total Carbs: 1.6g

MINI FRITTATAS

Preparation time: 5 minutes

Cooking time: 30 minutes

Servings: 12 muffins

Ingredients:

10 eggs

2 egg whites

8oz. pork sausage

1 cup green bell peppers, diced

1 cup red bell peppers, diced

½ cup Monterey Jack cheese, grated

½ cup milk

Salt and pepper, to taste

Directions:

Preheat oven to 350F.

Heat small amount of oil in skillet over medium-high heat. Remove pork sausage from the casing and cook until browned.

Remove the pork using slotted spoon and place aside. Cook the bell peppers in the same skillet until tender, for 5-6 minutes.

In a large bowl whisk the eggs with milk and egg whites. Divide the sausages and bell peppers between the 12-hole muffins tin.

Pour over the egg mixture, dividing evenly and sprinkle with cheese. Stir gently with fork and bake for 25-30 minutes. Place on wire rack to cool before removing from the tin. Serve after.

Nutritional Info: Per serving/muffin

Calories: 148

Cholesterol: 157mg

Protein: 10.6g

Total fat: 10.7g

Total Carbs: 2.4g

ZUCCHINI BREAD MUFFINS

Preparation time: 5 minutes

Cooking time: 25 minutes

Servings: 8

Ingredients:

4oz. zucchinis, grated

1 cup golden flaxseeds meal

1oz. vanilla whey protein

2 eggs

1/3 cup erythritol
2 teaspoons cinnamon
2 tablespoons butter
¾ teaspoon baking powder

1 pinch nutmeg
1 pinch all spice
1 teaspoon vanilla paste

Directions:

Preheat oven to 350F and line 8-hole muffin tin with paper cases.

Combine the eggs, oil and vanilla until smooth. Continue whisking until frothy.

Add grated zucchinis and stir.

Add the flaxseeds meal, protein powder, erythritol, baking powder and spices. Mix with spoon to combine.

Divide the mixture between paper cases and bake for 25 minutes. Allow to cool before removing from the tin.

Nutritional Info: Per serving/muffin

Calories: 120
Total fat: 8.4g

Cholesterol: 49mg
Total Carbs: 4.2g

Protein: 4.5g

CHEESE BAKED EGGS

Preparation time: 5 minutes   Cooking time: 10 minutes   Servings: 2

Ingredients:

2 tablespoons butter, unsalted
4 tablespoons heavy cream
4 tablespoons parmesan, grated

4 eggs
Salt and pepper, to taste

Directions:

Preheat oven to 357F.

Melt butter and use it to coat medium oven safe dish.

Combine the eggs and heavy cream and beat lightly.

Add grated cheese and season to taste.

Bake the eggs for 10 minutes and serve after, maybe with fresh chives or salad.

Nutritional Info: Per serving

Calories: 511
Total fat: 43.4g

Cholesterol: 339mg
Total Carbs: 3.5g

Protein: 29.8g

CABBAGE HASH BROWN

Preparation time: 5 minutes   Cooking time: 10 minutes   Servings: 2

Ingredients:

2 cup cabbage, Savoy, sliced thinly
1 green onion, sliced thinly
1 egg

1 tablespoon lard
Salt and pepper, to taste

Directions:

Combine the cabbage green onion, egg, salt and pepper in a bowl.

Stir until well combined.

Heat lard in large skillet over medium-high heat. Form 2 patties from the prepared mix and place into skillet. Cook until browned on the bottom and flip to the other side. Cook until browned and serve after.

Nutritional Info: Per serving

Calories: 100

Cholesterol: 97mg

Protein: 3.7g

Total fat: 8.0g

Total Carbs: 3.2g

COCONUT FRENCH TOAST

Preparation time: 5 minutes

Cooking time: 10 minutes

Servings: 2

Ingredients:

2 slices coconut bread

2 tablespoons butter

¼ cup water

1 tablespoon splenda

1 egg white

½ teaspoon cinnamon

Directions:

Whisk together the egg white, water and splenda until frothy.

Heat large non-stick skillet with butter over medium-high heat.

Dip coconut bread slices into egg white mixture and cook until browned.

Sprinkle with cinnamon before serving.

Nutritional Info: Per serving

Calories: 134

Cholesterol: 31mg

Protein: 3.9g

Total fat: 11.8g

Total Carbs: 3.1g

CINNAMON ROLL SCONES

Preparation time: 10 minutes

Cooking time: 25 minutes

Servings: 10

Ingredients:

2 cups almond flour

2 tablespoons heavy cream

1 egg

2 tablespoons erythritol

2 teaspoons baking powder

½ teaspoon baking soda

8 drops stevia

½ teaspoon cinnamon, ground

½ teaspoon baking soda

¼ cup coconut oil, melted

½ teaspoon vanilla paste

To sprinkle:

2 tablespoons erythritol

2 teaspoons cinnamon

Directions:

Preheat oven to 325F and line baking sheet with parchment paper.

In a bowl whisk the almond flour, baking powder, baking soda, erythritol and cinnamon.

In separate bowl whisk the egg, stevia, coconut oil and vanilla. Fold liquid ingredients into dry ones and stir until blended.

Transfer the dough onto baking sheet and shape into 8-inch circle, in diameter. Combine erythritol with cinnamon and sprinkle over prepare circle. Slice the circle into 8 wedges and bake in preheated oven for 25 minutes. Remove from the oven and place on wire rack to cool.
Serve after.

Nutritional Info: Per serving

Calories: 81	Cholesterol: 20mg	Protein: 1.2g
Total fat: 8.4g	Total Carbs: 1.3g	

CRUNCH CEREALS

Preparation time: 5 minutes	Cooking time: 20 minutes	Servings: 6

Ingredients:

3 tablespoon coconut oil, melted
½ cup hemp seeds, hulled
½ cup flax seeds, ground

2 tablespoons cinnamon
½ cup coconut water

Directions:

Combine all ingredients in a food blender. Process until blended thoroughly. Preheat oven to 300F and line baking sheet with parchment paper. Spread the batter over baking sheet to 1/16-inch thick layer.
Bake for 15 minutes at 300F and reduce heat to 250F and continue baking for 10 minutes more. Remove from the oven and cut into small squares. Place aside to cool.
To prepare the cereals; place ½ cup cereals into bowl and pour over the warmed coconut or almond milk. Serve and enjoy.

Nutritional Info: Per serving

Calories: 114	Cholesterol: 0mg	Protein: 1.8g
Total fat: 9.8g	Total Carbs: 3.5g	

SALAD SANDWICHES

Preparation time: 5 minutes	Servings: 2

Ingredients:

4 leaves cosmopolitan lettuce
4 cheese slices, any kind
¼ avocado

4oz. turkey ham
Salt and pepper, to taste

Directions:

Place lettuce leaves in front of you.
Top each lettuce leaf with cheese, turkey ham, avocado slices and finally tomato slices.
Season with taste and serve after.

Nutritional Info: Per serving

Calories: 345	Cholesterol: 95mg	Protein: 23.7g
Total fat: 25.7g	Total Carbs: 5.0g	

Coconut Cream with Berries

Preparation time: 5 minutes   Servings: 2

Ingredients:

1 cup coconut cream
1oz. blueberries

½ teaspoon vanilla paste

Directions:

Place the blueberries and vanilla paste in food blender.
Process until smooth.
Divide coconut cream between the bowls and top with processed berries. Serve after.

Nutritional Info: Per serving

Calories: 284   Cholesterol: 0mg   Protein: 2.9g
Total fat: 28.7g   Total Carbs: 5.7g

Avocado Breakfast Pudding

Preparation time: 5 minutes   Servings: 4

Ingredients:

1 avocado, peeled, stoned
½ cup almond milk

2 tablespoons almonds, crushed
1 tablespoon erythritol

Directions:

Blend avocado, milk, and erythritol in food blender until smooth.
Divide between two bowls and top with crushed almonds.
Chill for 30 minutes before serving.

Nutritional Info: Per serving

Calories: 189   Cholesterol: 0mg   Protein: 2.3g
Total fat: 18.4g   Total Carbs: 5.6g

Peppermint Cacao Shake

Preparation time: 5 minutes   Servings: 2

Ingredients:

1 cup cream cheese
2 cups water
4 tablespoons cacao powder, raw

½ cup vanilla protein powder
6 drops peppermint extract
1 ½ tablespoons eyrthritol

Directions:

In a food blender combine all ingredients by order.
Pulse until smooth and desired consistency is reached.
Serve in chilled glasses.

Nutritional Info: Per serving

Calories: 415

Cholesterol: 128mg

Protein: 9.3g

Total fat: 40.7g

Total Carbs: 4.6g

CHIA SEEDS AND ORANGE COOKIES

Preparation time: 5 minutes

Cooking time: 15 minutes

Servings: 12

Ingredients:

¼ cup coconut flour
1 tablespoon chia seeds
1 tablespoon orange zest
1 teaspoon lemon zest
2 tablespoons orange juice, fresh
1 tablespoon lemon juice, fresh

1 teaspoon baking powder
2 egg
4 tablespoons erythritol
2 scoops vanilla protein powder
1 teaspoon vanilla paste
2 tablespoons coconut oil, melted

Directions:

Preheat oven to 325F and line baking sheet with parchment paper. In a bowl combine the coconut flour, chia seeds, orange and lemon zest, baking powder, erythritol and vanilla protein powder.

In separate bowl whisk the orange and lemon juice, egg, vanilla paste and coconut oil. Stir in the coconut flour mixture and continue mixing until smooth. Place the cookie dough aside for 5 minutes.

Drop the cookie dough with ice cream scoop onto baking sheet. Flatten the dough to ¼-inch thickness and bake for 11-13 minutes. Place on wire rack to cool before serving.

Nutritional Info: Per serving

Calories: 32

Cholesterol: 14mg

Protein: 0.7g

Total fat: 2.8g

Total Carbs: 1.2g

SAVORY YOGURT BOWLS

Preparation time: 5 minutes

Servings: 2

Ingredients:

2 cups Greek yogurt
1oz. pine nuts
2 tablespoons extra-virgin olive oil

¼ cup feta cheese, crumbled
¼ teaspoon salt
½ teaspoon cayenne

Directions:

Heat large non-stick skillet over medium-high heat.

Add the pine nuts and toast for 1 minute; season with cayenne and toss to coat.

Divide yogurt between two bowls. Sprinkle with remaining olive oil, feta cheese and salt.

Top with toasted pine nuts and serve.

Nutritional Info: Per serving

Calories: 265

Cholesterol: 20.3mg

Protein: 15.3g

Total fat: 20.6g

Total Carbs: 5.1g

VEGETABLE PANCAKES

Preparation time: 5 minutes | Cooking time: 10 minutes | Servings: 12

Ingredients:

1 cup mashed cooked cauliflower
1 medium zucchini, grated
1 clove garlic, minced
3 tablespoons butter

Salt and pepper, to taste
¼ cup chives, chopped
2 eggs
1 tablespoon coconut flour

Directions:

In a bowl combine the cauliflower, zucchini, garlic and chives. Season with salt and pepper and place aside for 20 minutes. Squeeze the vegetables to remove excess liquid and crack in the eggs. Add coconut flour and stir the mixture until blended.
Heat butter in large skillet.
Form four patties from the mixture and place into skillet. Cook until browned, for 5 minutes. Flip the pancakes and cook for 3 minutes more. Serve after.

Nutritional Info: Per serving

Calories: 50
Total fat: 5.7g

Cholesterol: 37mg
Total Carbs: 1.2g

Protein: 1.4g

BANANA AND YOGURT MUFFINS

Preparation time: 5 minutes | Cooking time: 20 minutes | Servings: 14 muffins

Ingredients:

1 ¼ cup almond flour
½ cup coconut flour
¼ cup flaxseeds, ground
2 eggs
¼ cup yogurt
1 teaspoon baking soda

1 teaspoon baking powder
2 bananas, sliced
½ cup melted butter
¼ cup almonds, crushed
¼ cup erythritol

Directions:

In a food blender combine all ingredients except the crushed almonds.
Pulse until blended thoroughly.
Preheat oven to 350F and line 14-hole muffin tin with paper cases.
Divide the batter between paper cases and sprinkle on top with crushed walnuts.
Bake for 20-22 minutes and place on wire rack to cool for 5 minutes.
Remove the muffins from the tin and serve.

Nutritional Info: Per serving/muffin

Calories: 121
Total fat: 11.3g
Cholesterol: 41mg

Total Carbs: 4.6g
Protein: 2.1 g

MUSHROOMS SURPRISE

Preparation time: 5 minutes   Cooking time: 10 minutes   Servings: 2

Ingredients:

2 Portobello mushrooms
4 teaspoons olive oil
2 eggs
1 teaspoon garlic, minced

1 tablespoon cheddar cheese, grated
1 teaspoon thyme, dried, crushed
Salt and pepper, to taste

Directions:

Preheat oven to 400F.

Place the mushrooms on baking sheet lined with foil.

Sprinkle mushrooms with garlic and season to taste with salt and pepper.

Bake the mushrooms for 10 minutes.

Meanwhile, whisk the eggs and season to taste.

Heat the olive oil in skillet and cook the eggs over medium heat until cooked through.

When the mushrooms are baked, fill with prepared eggs. Sprinkle on top with grated cheese and crushed thyme. Serve immediately.

Nutritional Info: Per serving/muffin

Calories: 171
Total fat: 14.9g

Cholesterol: 167mg
Total Carbs: 2.7g

Protein: 8.1 g

BREAKFAST DELI WRAPS

Preparation time: 15 minutes   Servings: 2

Ingredients:

4 slices black forest deli ham
6 slices Genoa salami
2 tablespoons mayonnaise
1 cup coleslaw mix

½ teaspoon milk
1 teaspoon vinegar, white
4 slices cheese – by your choice
1 teaspoon Erythritol

Directions:

Combine the mayonnaise, vinegar, milk, and Erythritol in a bowl.

Add coleslaw and toss to combine.

Place 2 slices of ham in front of you so they are slightly overlapping.

Place on top with 3 slices salami and two slices cheese.

Repeat with remaining ham, salami and cheese. Spread over coleslaw mix and roll.

Serve after.

Nutritional Info: Per serving

Calories: 267
Total fat: 20.4g
Cholesterol: 40mg

Total Carbs: 10.5g
Protein: 6.7g

HAM AND MELON WRAPS

Preparation time: 15 minutes　　　Servings: 4

Ingredients:

8 slices deli ham
8oz. cream cheese
2oz. melon chunks

1 teaspoon hot sauce
8 kale leaves

Directions:

In a food blender blend the cream cheese, hot sauce and melon.
Place two pieces of deli ham in front of you so they are slightly overlapping.
Repeat with remaining ham. Spread over prepared cream cheese mix and top with kale leaves.
Roll up and serve.

Nutritional Info: Per serving

Calories: 289
Total fat: 24.6g

Cholesterol: 94mg
Total Carbs: 3.7g

Protein: 13.6g

ASPARAGUS AND HAM ROLL

Preparation time: 10 minutes　　Cooking time: 5 minutes　　Servings: 4

Ingredients:

8 slices ham, cut in half lengthwise
16 asparagus spears
1 red bell pepper, cut into 16 strips

8 oz. cheese like Gouda, cut into 16 slices
Pepper – to taste

Directions:

Place asparagus in sauce pan and add just enough water to cover.
Simmer for 3 minutes over medium heat; drain and place aside.
Place ham slices in front of you; top each with asparagus, cheese and bell pepper slice/piece.
Roll up tightly and serve.

Nutritional Info: Per serving

Calories: 319
Total fat: 20.4g

Cholesterol: 96mg
Total Carbs: 8.3g

Protein: 25.7g

SALAMI AND CHEESE ROLLS

Preparation time: 20 minutes　　　Servings: 8

Ingredients:

1lb. cream cheese
¾ lb. salami, thinly sliced
½ green bell pepper, sliced into thin strips

Directions:

Place a piece of plastic foil on working surface.

Place the cheese onto plastic foil and cover with another piece. Roll the cheese to ¼-inch thick and remove the upper foil layer. Top the cheese with salami slices so they are overlapping slightly.

Place the foil over salami and carefully flip so the cheese is on top and salami on bottom. Remove the foil from the cheese layer and top with bell pepper.

Roll the salami using the foil to make it tight as possible. Refrigerate the log for 2 hours. Unwrap after 2 hours and slice before serving.

Nutritional Info: Per serving

Calories: 311
Total fat: 29.2g

Cholesterol: 93mg
Total Carbs: 2.9g

Protein: 9.7g

CHEESE AND GARLIC ROLLS

Preparation time: 15 minutes   Servings: 8

Ingredients:

3 tablespoons mayonnaise
2 clove garlic, minced
10oz. ham, sliced

10oz. Gouda cheese, grated
1 tablespoon chives, fresh, chopped

Directions:

In a bowl combine the cheese, chives, mayonnaise and garlic.
Place one tablespoon of prepared mixture onto a ham slice.
Roll tightly and serve after.

Nutritional Info: Per serving

Calories: 205
Total fat: 14.5g

Cholesterol: 62mg
Total Carbs: 2.7g

Protein: 14.7g

CREAM CHEESE PANCAKES

Preparation time: 5 minutes   Cooking time: 10 minutes   Servings: 2

Ingredients:

4 oz. cream cheese
2 tablespoon almond flour
Stevia to taste

4 eggs, whisked
1 teaspoon cinnamon

Directions:

In a food blender combine the cream cheese, almond flour, eggs, cinnamon and stevia.
Pulse until blended thoroughly.
Meanwhile, heat non-stick skillet with small amount of cooking oil over medium-high heat.
Place ¼ of pancake batter in the skillet and cook for 2 minutes or until bubbles appear.
Flip carefully and cook for 30 seconds more. Serve after.

Nutritional Info: Per serving

Calories: 327

Total fat: 28.5g

Cholesterol: 290mg

Total Carbs: 3.1g

Protein: 15.4g

KETO PANCAKE DONUTS

Preparation time: 5 minutes

Cooking time: 10 minutes

Servings: 6

Ingredients:

4 tablespoons almond flour

1 teaspoon vanilla extract

3 eggs

3oz. cream cheese

1 tablespoon coconut flour

1 teaspoon baking powder

4 tablespoons Erythritol

Directions:

In a food blender place all ingredients.

Process until smooth and well combined.

Heat the donut maker and spray with some cooking oil. Pour in batter until almost full.

Cook for 3 minutes, flip and cook for 2 minutes more.

Remove donuts, repeat with remaining batter and serve with bacon.

Nutritional Info: Per serving

Calories: 110

Total fat: 9.5g

Cholesterol: 97mg

Total Carbs: 2.0g

Protein: 4.8g

COCOA PANCAKES

Preparation time: 5 minutes

Cooking time: 10 minutes

Servings: 6

Ingredients:

3 tablespoons raw cocoa

1 tablespoon coconut oil, melted

3 eggs

3oz. cream cheese

1 bananas, mashed

Directions:

Place the banana mash in food blender; add eggs, and cheese, and pulse until smooth.

Add cocoa powder and coconut oil; process until blended thoroughly.

Heat non-stick skillet over medium-high heat. Add 3-4 tablespoons of batter into skillet and cook for 4 minutes. Flip and cook for 2 minutes more.

Serve after.

Nutritional Info: Per serving

Calories: 134

Total fat: 10.5g

Cholesterol:125mg

Total Carbs: 4.6g

Protein: 5.5g

$\mathcal{P}$UMPKIN PANCAKES

Preparation time: 5 minutes   Cooking time: 10 minutes   Servings: 4

Ingredients:
1 cup almond flour
1 teaspoon all-spice
1 teaspoon baking powder
3 tablespoons ghee

¼ cup pumpkin puree
¼ cup sour cream
1 pinch salt
2 eggs, whole

Directions:
Mix the eggs, sour cream and pumpkin puree until smooth.
In separate bowl whisk the almond flour, baking powder, all-spice and salt.
Gradually add dry ingredients in liquid ones and stir until combined.
Grease skillet with some ghee. Once the skillet is hot and 1/3 cup pancake mixture per pancake.
Cook the pancakes until bubbles appear on surface; flip and cook for 2 minutes.
Serve after while still hot.

Nutritional Info: Per serving
Calories: 193   Cholesterol: 113mg   Protein: 4.9g
Total fat: 18.3g   Total Carbs: 4.1g

$\mathcal{W}$ALNUT PANCAKES

Preparation time: 5 minutes   Cooking time: 10 minutes   Servings: 4

Ingredients:
½ cup walnuts, chopped
½ cup almond milk
4 eggs
2 tablespoons Erythritol
1 teaspoon baking powder

1 cup almond flour
1 tablespoon coconut flour
½ teaspoon cinnamon, ground
4 tablespoons walnut oil

Directions:
In a bowl whisk together the almond flour, coconut flour, cinnamon and baking powder.
Stir in the walnut oil, eggs, almond milk and chopped walnuts.
Heat large non-stick skillet over medium heat; add some cooking oil.
Once the oil is hot pour ¼ cup batter per pancake. Cook the pancakes until edges are set and bottom is brown.
Flip carefully and cook for 2 minutes.
Serve the pancakes while still hot.

Nutritional Info: Per serving
Calories: 279   Cholesterol: 164mg   Protein: 11.9g
Total fat: 25.4g   Total Carbs: 5.1g

Avocado Vanilla Smoothie

Preparation time: 5 minutes   Servings: 2

Ingredients:

¼ avocado, peeled, stoned
1 ¼ cups ice
2 tablespoons almond butter
½ cup almond milk

1 cup heavy cream
1 pinch cinnamon
½ teaspoon vanilla paste

Directions:

Combine all ingredients in food blender. Process until smooth and serve immediately.

Nutritional Info: Per serving

Calories: 495   Cholesterol: 82mg   Protein: 6.5g
Total fat: 50.4g   Total Carbs: 9.3g

Chocolate Smoothie

Preparation time: 5 minutes   Servings: 1

Ingredients:

2 eggs, free - range
1 tablespoon coconut oil
½ cup ice
½ cup water

1 tablespoon cacao powder
3 drops stevia
¼ cup coconut milk
½ teaspoon cinnamon

Directions:

Place all ingredients in food blender. Process until smooth and serve after.

Nutritional Info: Per serving

Calories: 384   Cholesterol: 227mg   Protein: 12.5g
Total fat: 36.7g   Total Carbs: 4.9g

Banana and Peanut Butter Smoothie

Preparation time: 5 minutes   Servings: 2

Ingredients:

2 tablespoons chia seeds
1 cup heavy cream
½ cup almond milk or plain milk

½ pcs banana, sliced
2 tablespoons peanut butter
10 drops stevia

Directions:

In a blender combine all ingredients by order. Blend until smooth and serve after.

Nutritional Info: Per serving

Calories: 358

Cholesterol: 87mg

Protein: 7.5g

Total fat: 31.6g

Total Carbs: 9.9g

MELON BREAKFAST SMOOTHIE

Preparation time: 5 minutes

Servings: 2

Ingredients:

1 cup heavy cream

½ cup melon, chopped

¼ cup water

½ banana, sliced

1 tablespoon coconut oil, melted, virgin

Directions:

In a blender place all ingredients. Pulse until blended thoroughly and smooth. Serve after.

Nutritional Info: Per serving

Calories: 305

Cholesterol: 82mg

Protein: 1.9g

Total fat: 29.2g

Total Carbs: 8.6g

CHEESECAKE SMOOTHIE

Preparation time: 5 minutes

Servings: 1

Ingredients:

½ cup raspberries, fresh

5 drops stevia

½ cup water

¼ cup heavy whipping cream

1 tablespoon coconut oil, melted, virgin

¼ teaspoon vanilla powder

¼ cup coconut milk, creamed

Directions:

In a blender combine all ingredients. Process until smooth. Serve after.

Nutritional Info: Per serving

Calories: 391

Cholesterol: 41mg

Protein: 2.7g

Total fat: 39.4g

Total Carbs: 9.5g

HEMP PORRIDGE

Preparation time: 5 minutes

Cooking time: 5 minutes

Servings: 2

Ingredients:

1 cup heavy cream

2 tablespoon almond flour

1 tablespoon chia seeds

5 drops stevia

½ cup hemp hearts

¼ cup almonds, ground

1 teaspoon vanilla paste

1 tablespoon nuts - by your choice

½ teaspoon cinnamon, ground

Directions:

Combine the heavy cream, chia sees, hemp hearts, vanilla, cinnamon, almond flour, and stevia in a small sauce pan.

Heat over medium heat until just starts to boil. Once bubbly, stir once and cook for 1-2 minutes.

Remove from the heat and stir in ground almonds. Serve in a bowl and top with nuts by your choice.

Nutritional Info: Per serving

Calories: 303	Cholesterol: 82mg	Protein: 4.5g
Total fat: 30.4g	Total Carbs: 5.8g	

Quick "Oatmeal"

Preparation time: 10 minutes	Cooking time: 5 minutes	Servings: 2

Ingredients:

¼ cup coconut, shredded and unsweetened
1 teaspoon vanilla extract
1/3 cup almonds, flaked
1 teaspoon vanilla paste
2 tablespoons Erythritol

2 tablespoons chia seeds
½ cup heavy cream, warmed
1 cup water, warm
½ cup blackberries
5 drops stevia

Directions:

Place the chia seeds, almond flakes, coconut and Erythritol in a bowl. Add warmed heavy cream, water, vanilla and stevia.

Stir well to combine and place side for 10 minutes.

Top with blackberries.

Nutritional Info: Per serving

Calories: 252	Cholesterol: 41mg	Protein: 4.8g
Total fat: 22.5g	Total Carbs: 8.5g	

Squash Bowl

Preparation time: 5 minutes	Servings: 4

Ingredients:

1 cup coconut, shredded
½ banana, sliced
½ cup squash puree

½ cup heavy cream
1 teaspoon cinnamon
2 apricots, chopped

Directions:

Process the ingredients in a food processor until combined.

Spoon onto serving bowls and top with chopped apricots.

Nutritional Info: Per serving

Calories: 135	Cholesterol: 21mg	Protein: 1.4g
Total fat: 12.4g	Total Carbs: 6.3g	

APPLE-CINNAMON BREAKFAST BOWL

Preparation time: 5 minutes   Cooking time: 10 minutes   Servings: 2

Ingredients:

1 cup cauliflower "rice", (just process cauliflower florets in food processor)
1 teaspoon cinnamon, ground
2 tablespoons pecans, chopped
2 eggs, whisked

2 tablespoons almond meal
1/3 cup apple cider
1/3 cup heavy cream
¼ teaspoon nutmeg

Directions:

Place cauliflower "rice" and pecans in sauce pan.
Add heavy cream, cider vinegar and spices.
Bring to boil and once bubbly reduce heat; cook for 10 minutes.
Remove from the heat and whisk in the eggs, in steady stream.
Add almond meal and continue mixing until combined. Serve immediately.

Nutritional Info: Per serving

Calories: 168   Cholesterol: 191mg   Protein: 7.0g
Total fat: 12.0g   Total Carbs: 8.5g

BANANA NUT BOWL

Preparation time: 25 minutes   Servings: 4

Ingredients:

1 cup heavy cream
2 tablespoons butter
1 banana, sliced
¼ cup cashews, raw

¼ cup pecans, raw
¼ cup almonds, raw
1 teaspoon cinnamon
Stevia - to taste

Directions:

To prepare the nuts; place the nuts in a bowl and cover with water. Soak overnight.
Drain the nuts in the morning and rinse until water runs clear.
Place the nuts in food processor; add the heavy cream, butter, banana and cinnamon.
Pulse until blended and smooth. Divide the mixture between two microwave safe bowl and microwave on high for 40 seconds.
Remove and top with raisins.

Nutritional Info: Per serving

Calories: 266   Cholesterol: 56mg   Protein: 3.6g
Total fat: 23.9g   Total Carbs: 10.1g

SCALLION FRITTATA

Preparation time: 5 minutes   Cooking time: 15 minutes   Servings: 4

Ingredients:

4 eggs
1oz. Parmesan, grated
1 ½ tablespoons olive oil
3 scallions, sliced
1 pinch pepper, black

1 ½ tablespoons milk
1 pinch salt
2 cups arugula
2 oz. goat cheese, crumbled

Directions:

Preheat oven to 375F.

Heat olive oil in skillet over medium-high heat; add scallions and cook until tender.

Meanwhile, whisk the eggs with salt, parmesan, pepper and milk.

Pour the eggs over scallions and stir.

Pop the eggs into oven and bake for 15 minutes or until set. Serve with arugula and top with goat cheese.

Nutritional Info: Per serving

Calories: 204
Total fat: 16.4g

Cholesterol: 184mg
Total Carbs: 2.4g

Protein: 12.8g

SKILLET SOUFFLÉ

Preparation time: 5 minutes   Cooking time: 10 minutes   Servings: 4

Ingredients:

6 eggs, separated
4oz. goats cheese
2 tablespoon olive oil
¼ cup chives, chopped

½ teaspoon salt
1pinch black pepper
1 tablespoon butter

Directions:

Heat oven to 400F.

In a bowl whisk together the egg yolks, salt, pepper and chives.

In separate bowl whisk the egg whites until soft peaks form.

Gently fold the egg whites in egg yolk mixture.

Melt the butter in skillet over medium-high heat. Add the egg mixture to the skillet and top with crumbled cheese. Bake until puffed over medium heat for 10 minutes.

Serve warm.

Nutritional Info: Per serving

Calories: 219
Total fat: 19.0g

Cholesterol: 253mg
Total Carbs: 2.4g

Protein: 10.6g

*E*GGS WITH HERBS

Preparation time: 5 minutes   Cooking time: 10 minutes   Servings: 4

Ingredients:

8 eggs
2 tablespoons milk
1 pinch salt
1 pinch pepper

1 ½ tablespoon butter
¼ cup parsley
¼ cup tarragon

Directions:

Heat butter in skillet over medium heat. In a bowl whisk the eggs with milk, salt and pepper.
Pour into the pan, add the herbs and cook until reach desired doneness. Serve after.

Nutritional Info: Per serving

Calories: 175   Cholesterol: 199mg   Protein: 11.9g
Total fat: 13.4g   Total Carbs: 2.2g

*B*AKED EGG WITH CREAM

Preparation time: 5 minutes   Cooking time: 20 minutes   Servings: 4

Ingredients:

8 eggs
8 tablespoons heavy cream
1 pinch salt

1 pinch pepper
1 tablespoon dill, chopped

Directions:

Heat oven to 400F and grease four ramekins with some butter.
Place 2 tablespoons cream in each ramekin. Crack 2 eggs in each ramekin and season with salt and pepper.
Bake for 20 minutes and sprinkle with dill before serving.

Nutritional Info: Per serving

Calories: 231   Cholesterol: 368mg   Protein: 11.8g
Total fat: 19.9g   Total Carbs: 2.0g

*A*VOCADOS STUFFED WITH EGGS

Preparation time: 5 minutes   Cooking time: 20 minutes   Servings: 4

Ingredients:

8 eggs
4 avocados, halved

4oz. smoked salmon, cut into strips
Salt and pepper – to taste

Directions:

Preheat oven to 425F. Halve the avocados and remove the seeds.
Arrange avocados onto baking sheet and line the hollows with smoked salmon strips.

Crack eggs carefully in a bowl so eggs yolks remain whole. Lift the egg yolks and place into avocado; add around as much as egg whites as avocado can hold. Season with salt and pepper. Pop in the oven and bake for 15-20 minutes.
Serve after.

Nutritional Info: Per serving

Calories: 569
Total fat: 49.2g

Cholesterol: 334mg
Total Carbs: 16.0g

Protein: 20.1g

BANANA PARFAIT

Preparation time: 5 minutes

Servings: 1

Ingredients:

1 cup whipped heavy cream
¼ cup walnuts, crushed
½ teaspoon cinnamon

¼ small banana, sliced
2 drops stevia

Directions:

In a bowl combine the whipped cream, cinnamon and stevia.
Place 1/3 of the walnut in bottom of glass.
Top with 1/3 Greek yogurt mix and some banana slices. Repeat the layers until you are out of ingredients.
Serve immediately.

Nutritional Info: Per serving

Calories: 486
Total fat: 50.3g

Cholesterol: 164mg
Total Carbs: 6.8g

Protein: 5.0g

PISTACHIO PARFAIT

Preparation time: 5 minutes

Servings: 2

Ingredients:

¼ cup pistachios
1 cup ricotta
¼ cup cream cheese
¼ teaspoon vanilla

¼ teaspoon almond extract
1pcs kiwi, peeled, diced
5 drops stevia

Directions:

In a bowl combine the ricotta with extracts cream cheese, and stevia.
Divide half of the ricotta mix between two parfait glasses.
Top with pistachios and kiwi and second layer of ricotta mix.
Chill before serving.

Nutritional Info: Per serving

Calories: 397
Total fat: 31.8g

Cholesterol: 102mg
Total Carbs: 7.5g

Protein: 19.2g

*I*SLAND BREAKFAST PARFAIT

Preparation time: 5 minutes + inactive time   Servings: 2

Ingredients:

6 tablespoons chia seeds
2 cups heavy cream
5 drops stevia
¼ teaspoon cinnamon

1/8 teaspoon vanilla
½ cup blackberries
4 tablespoons coconut flakes, toasted
2 tablespoons pistachios, chopped

Directions:

Prepare chia in advance; combine (6 hours before serving) the chia seeds, heavy cream, stevia, cinnamon and vanilla in a food processor. Pulse until blended and place in fridge for 6 hours.
30 minutes before serving stir in half of the blackberries.
When ready to serve, divide the chia mix between the parfait glasses. Top with pistachios, coconut and remaining blackberries. Serve and enjoy.

Nutritional Info: Per serving

Calories: 501   Cholesterol: 164mg   Protein: 4.8g
Total fat: 50.9g   Total Carbs: 11.1g

*P*UMPKIN PARFAIT

Preparation time: 5 minutes   Servings: 2

Ingredients:

¼ cup pumpkin puree
½ cup cream cheese
2 tablespoons almond milk

4 tablespoons chia seeds
1 tablespoon coconut flakes, toasted
3 drops stevia

Directions:

In a food processor combine the cheese, pumpkin puree and chia seeds.
Pulse few times. Add almond milk and stevia and pulse until blended.
Serve into bowl and sprinkle with toasted coconut.

Nutritional Info: Per serving

Calories: 256   Cholesterol: 64mg   Protein: 5.1g
Total fat: 24.7g   Total Carbs: 5.2g

*M*ANGO AND COCONUT CHIA PARFAIT

Preparation time: 5 minutes + inactive time   Servings: 2

Ingredients:

3 tablespoon chia seeds

1 cup heavy cream

1 pinch cinnamon
4 tablespoons coconut cream

¼ cup mango, peeled, diced
¼ teaspoon vanilla extract

Directions:

Combine the chia seeds with heavy cream and cinnamon in bowl. Cover and place aside for 3 hours.
Place the mango in food blender and process until smooth.
Combine coconut cream with vanilla in a bowl.
Assemble the parfait; divide the chia seeds mix between the parfait glasses.
Top with mango puree, and coconut-vanilla cream. Serve after.

Nutritional Info: Per serving

Calories: 303
Total fat: 29.5g

Cholesterol: 82mg
Total Carbs: 9.8g

Protein: 2.3g

CLASSIC PEANUT BUTTER SMOOTHIE

Preparation time: 5 minutes   Servings: 2

Ingredients:

1 cup heavy cream
½ cup cottage cheese
2 tablespoons peanut butter

2 tablespoons coconut oil
1 cup ice cubes
4 drops liquid stevia

Directions:

Combine all ingredients in a food blender. Blend on high until smooth.
Serve immediately.

Nutritional Info: Per serving

Calories: 469
Total fat: 44.9g

Cholesterol: 87mg
Total Carbs: 6.9g

Protein: 13.0g

VANILLA SMOOTHIE

Preparation time: 5 minutes   Servings: 1

Ingredients:

2 tablespoons almond butter
½ cup cream cheese
1 teaspoon vanilla paste

½ tablespoon coconut oil, melted
½ cup water
3 drops liquid stevia

Directions:

Combine all ingredients in a food blender. Blend on high until smooth.
Serve after.

Nutritional Info: Per serving

Calories: 659
Total fat: 65.2g

Cholesterol: 128mg
Total Carbs: 9.1g

Protein: 15.6g

FLUFFY SMOOTHIE

Preparation time: 5 minutes   Servings: 2

Ingredients:

4oz. egg whites
1/3 cup milk
½ cup heavy cream

1 teaspoon vanilla paste
6 drops stevia

Directions:

Combine all ingredients in a food blender.
Blend on high until smooth.
Serve after.

Nutritional Info: Per serving

Calories: 119   Cholesterol: 44mg   Protein: 8.1g
Total fat: 12.1g   Total Carbs: 3.2g

MELON COTTAGE SMOOTHIE

Preparation time: 5 minutes   Servings: 2

Ingredients:

1 cup cottage cheese
½ cup melon
1 cup almond milk

3 tablespoons coconut oil
8 drops liquid stevia

Directions:

Combine all ingredients in a food blender.
Blend on high until smooth.
Serve after.

Nutritional Info: Per serving

Calories: 567   Cholesterol: 9mg   Protein: 18.5g
Total fat: 51.3g   Total Carbs: 10.6g

CHEDDAR HAM SOUFFLÉ

Preparation time: 5 minutes   Cooking time: 20 minutes   Servings: 6

Ingredients:

¼ cup olive oil
3 teaspoons garlic, minced
6 eggs
7oz. ham
½ cup heavy cream

1 ¼ cups Cheddar cheese, grated
2 tablespoons chopped chives
Salt and pepper, to taste

Directions:

Heat oven to 400Fand prepare six ramekins.

Heat the oil in a skilled and add the garlic.

Cook until fragrant, for 1 minute.

In a bowl, combine the eggs, ham, heavy cream, cheddar cheese, chives, salt, and pepper.

Add the garlic, with olive oil and stir to combine.

Spoon the mixture into ramekins and bake for 20 minutes.

Serve after.

Nutritional Info: Per serving

Calories: 321

Total fat: 27.1g

Cholesterol: 221mg

Total Carbs: 2.7g

Protein: 17.2g

MINI SAUSAGE THYME PIES

Preparation time: 10 minutes   Cooking time: 25 minutes   Servings: 4 mini pies

Ingredients:

2 chicken sausages, smoked (or pork sausages)

1 cup cheddar cheese, grated

5 large egg yolks

¼ cup melted coconut oil

¼ cup coconut flour

2 tablespoons water

½ teaspoon dried thyme

2 teaspoons lemon juice

¼ teaspoon baking soda

1 pinch red pepper flakes

Salt and pepper, to taste

Directions:

Heat oven to 375F/180C and prepare four mini pie ramekins.

Heat the non-stick skillet over medium-high heat.

Brush with coconut oil and fry the chopped sausage until browned. Remove from the heat.

In a bowl, combine half the cheddar cheese, coconut flour, thyme, salt, pepper, baking soda, and red pepper flakes.

In a separate bowl, whisk the egg yolks until almost pale. Add the water, lemon juice, and coconut oil. Beat until blended.

Fold in the dry ingredients and stir until combined.

Transfer the dough into ramekins and top with sausages and remaining cheese. Bake the mini pies for 25 minutes.

Serve after.

Nutritional Info: Per serving/pie

Calories: 219

Total fat: 17.4g

Cholesterol: 297mg

Total Carbs: 3.3g

Protein: 12.2g

Scotch Eggs with Parmesan

Preparation time: 10 minutes   Cooking time: 10 minutes   Servings: 4

Ingredients:

4 hardboiled eggs, peeled
2 large eggs, whisked
¼ cup Parmesan cheese
¼ cup almond flour

8 slices bacon
1 tablespoon olive oil
2 tablespoons melted coconut oil

Directions:

In a bowl, combine the parmesan cheese and almond flour.
In a separate bowl, whisk the eggs, with a pinch of salt if preferred.
Wrap the eggs with 2 slices bacon per egg, one slice horizontally, one vertically.
Heat the olive oil and coconut oil in a skillet.
Dip the wrapped eggs into eggs, then parmesan mixture, shake off the excess.
Place the eggs into heated oil and fry until fully browned, all sides.
Transfer the eggs onto paper towels to drain.
Serve after.

Nutritional Info: Per serving

Calories: 433
Total fat: 36.5g

Cholesterol: 298mg
Total Carbs: 2.6g

Protein: 24.3g

Black Deli Wraps

Preparation time: 5 minutes   Servings: 2

Ingredients:

4 slices black forest deli ham(dry cured smoked ham)
6 slices Genoa salami, pork or beef
2 tablespoons mayonnaise
1 cup coleslaw mix

1 teaspoon cream
1 teaspoon vinegar, white
4 slices Gouda cheese
1 teaspoon Erythritol

Directions:

Combine the mayonnaise, vinegar, cream, and Erythritol in a bowl.
Add coleslaw and toss to combine.
Place 2 slices of ham in front of you so they are slightly overlapping.
Place on top with 3 slices salami and two slices cheese.
Repeat with remaining ham, salami and cheese. Spread over coleslaw mix and roll.
Serve after.

Nutritional Info: Per serving

Calories: 317
Total fat: 19.6g

Cholesterol: 83mg
Total Carbs: 4.8g

Protein: 20.9g

Vanilla Bacon Pancake Donuts

Preparation time: 5 minutes   Cooking time: 5 minutes   Servings: 6 donuts

Ingredients:

¼ cup almond flour
1 teaspoon vanilla paste
3 large eggs
4oz. cream cheese

1 tablespoon coconut flour
1 teaspoon baking powder
4 tablespoons Erythritol
3 slices bacon, cooked crumbled

Directions:

In a food blender, combine the almond flour, vanilla, eggs, cream cheese, coconut flour, baking powder, and Erythritol. Blend until smooth and well combined.
Heat the donut maker and spray with some cooking oil. Pour in batter until almost full.
Cook for 3 minutes, flip, and cook for 2 minutes.
Remove donuts, repeat with remaining batter and serve with bacon.

Nutritional Info: Per serving

Calories: 129   Cholesterol:114mg   Protein: 5.6g
Total fat: 11.4g   Total Carbs: 2.1g

Egg smoothie

Preparation time: 5 minutes   Servings: 2

Ingredients:

1 ½ cups heavy cream
½ cup water
2 tablespoons peanut butter

3 tablespoons heavy cream
1 pasteurized egg
6 drops liquid stevia

Directions:

Combine all ingredients in a food blender. Blend on high until smooth. Serve after.

Nutritional Info: Per serving

Calories: 414   Cholesterol: 221mg   Protein: 8.7g
Total fat: 40.8g   Total Carbs: 6.0g

Peachy Smoothie

Preparation time: 5 minutes   Servings: 1

Ingredients:

1 cup heavy cream
¼ almond milk
1 cup cottage cheese
1 medium peach, pitted

3 drops stevia
2 tablespoons coconut oil
½ teaspoon vanilla paste

Directions:

In a food blender combine all the ingredients. Blend on high until smooth. Serve after.

Nutritional Info: Per serving

Calories: 426   Cholesterol: 91mg   Protein: 16.8g
Total fat: 38.0g   Total Carbs: 5.8g

ALMOND CACAO SMOOTHIE

Preparation time: 5 minutes   Servings: 2

Ingredients:

1 cup water   3 drops liquid stevia
1 cup heavy cream   ¼ cup cream cheese
1 tablespoon cacao   1 tablespoon almond butter

Directions:

Combine all ingredients in a food blender. Blend on high until smooth. Serve after.

Nutritional Info: Per serving

Calories: 357   Cholesterol: 114mg   Protein: 5.1g
Total fat: 36.8g   Total Carbs: 3.9g

LIME AVOCADO SMOOTHIE

Preparation time: 5 minutes   Servings: 2

Ingredients:

1 cup cream cheese   1 ½ tablespoons olive oil
1 cup water   2 tablespoons basil
¼ avocado   1 lime, juiced
2 tablespoons water

Directions:

Peel and pit the avocado. Place in a food blender. Add the remaining ingredients and blend until smooth. Serve after.

Nutritional Info: Per serving

Calories: 547   Cholesterol: 128mg   Protein: 9.3g
Total fat: 55.9g   Total Carbs: 5.3g

GREEN KIWI SMOOTHIE

Preparation time: 5 minutes   Servings: 1

Ingredients:

1 cup heavy cream
¾ cup cottage cheese
½ kiwi fruits, peeled   1/8 avocado, peeled, pitted
½ cup romaine lettuce   3 drops stevia

Directions:

Combine all ingredients in a food blender.
Blend on high until smooth.
Serve after.

Nutritional Info: Per serving

Calories: 645   Cholesterol: 178mg   Protein: 28.8g
Total fat: 52.8g   Total Carbs: 18.1g

STRAWBERRY CHEESE SMOOTHIE

Preparation time: 5 minutes   Servings: 2

Ingredients:

¼ cup strawberries, sliced
¾ cup cream cheese
1 cup milk, full-fat   ½ teaspoon vanilla paste
1 tablespoon coconut oil   3 drops stevia

Directions:

Combine all ingredients in a food blender.
Blend on high until smooth,
Serve after.

Nutritional Info: Per serving

Calories: 429   Cholesterol: 106mg   Protein: 10.7g
Total fat: 39.7g   Total Carbs: 8.7g

Lunch and Dinner recipes

Green Turkey Salad

Preparation time: 10 minutes   Servings: 2

Ingredients:

6oz. grilled turkey dark meat, sliced
2 cups arugula
¼ avocado, peeled, sliced
1 cup baby spinach
¼ cup pumpkin seeds

For the dressing:
1 garlic clove, minced
2 tablespoons lemon juice
¼ teaspoon salt
1 pinch ground pepper
1 tablespoon raw cider vinegar
1 teaspoon mustard

Directions:

Prepare the dressing: in a mini blender combine all the dressing ingredients.
Blend until smooth.
Prepare the salad: toss the grilled turkey, arugula, baby spinach, pumpkin seeds, and avocado in a bowl.
Pour over prepared dressing and toss gently. Serve immediately

Nutritional Info: Per serving

Calories: 275
Total fat: 18.3g

Cholesterol: 59mg
Total Carbs: 8.0g

Protein: 23.4g

Aromatic Pork Tenderloin

Preparation Time: 10 minutes   Cooking time: 20 minutes   Servings: 4

Ingredients:

1lb. pork tenderloin
1 tablespoon fresh rosemary, copped
1 teaspoon garlic powder
1 teaspoon lemon zest

4 tablespoons melted butter
½ teaspoon salt
¼ teaspoon black pepper

Directions:

Preheat oven to 400F.
Preheat the grill pan over-medium-high heat.
Brush the pork tenderloin with melted butter, on all sides. Sprinkle with salt, pepper, fresh rosemary, and orange zest.
Sear the pork tenderloin in a grill pan for 2 minute per side. This way the pork will keep all the juices inside.
Transfer into a baking dish and bake for 18-20 minutes.
Remove from the oven and let the pork rest before slicing and serving.

Nutritional Info: Per serving

Calories: 270

Total fat: 15.6g

Cholesterol: 113mg

Total Carbs: 1.2g

Protein: 30.0g

TURKEY AND ZUCCHINI BURGERS

Preparation Time: 10 minutes

Cooking Time: 10 minutes

Servings: 4 burgers

Ingredients:

1lb. ground turkey
1 cup grated zucchini, liquid squeezed
1 medium egg
2 tablespoons chopped flat-leaf parsley
2 tablespoons chopped coriander
2 garlic cloves, minced
½ teaspoon ground cumin

½ teaspoon salt
¼ teaspoon black pepper

For the lime sauce:

7oz. Greek yogurt
1 tablespoon olive oil
1 lime, juiced
Salt and pepper, to taste

Directions:

Squeeze the grated zucchini to remove excess liquid.

Combine the zucchini with minced turkey, egg, parsley, coriander, garlic, and cumin. Season to taste and stir until blended thoroughly.

Meanwhile, prepare the sauce: combine all the sauce ingredients in a bowl. Chill until ready to use. Preheat the grill.

Form four patties form the prepared mixture. Grill for 5 minutes per side.

Serve burgers, drizzled with sauce, and with toasted buns.

Nutritional Info: Per serving

Calories: 313

Total fat: 18.2g

Cholesterol: 159mg

Total Carbs: 3.9g

Protein: 32.0g

SALMON WITH STIR-FRIED SALAD

Preparation Time: 5 minutes

Cooking Time: 10 minutes

Servings: 4

Ingredients:

4 4oz.salmon fillets, skin on
2 tablespoons olive oil
2 tablespoon coconut aminos
1 teaspoon chopped ginger
2 green bell peppers, sliced

1 red chili pepper, seeded and chopped
2 cups baby spinach
2 tablespoons coriander leaves
¼ teaspoon salt
1/8 teaspoon black pepper

Directions:

In a bowl, combine the ½ tablespoon oil, coconut aminos, chopped ginger, and chili pepper. Preheat the grill. Brush the salmon fillets with oil and season to taste.

Grill over 500F, for total 8 minutes, starting with the skin down.
Heat the remaining sesame oil in the pan. Once hot, add the bell peppers and coriander.
Stir-fry for 1-2 minutes over medium-high heat. Remove from the heat and stir in the spinach.
Pour over prepared soy dressing and toss to combine.
Serve with prepared salmon.

Nutritional Info: Per serving

Calories: 235

Cholesterol: 50mg

Protein: 23.1g

Total fat: 14.2g

Total Carbs: 5.5g

Chicken Meatballs with Cheese

Preparation Time: 5 minutes
Cooking Time: 12 minutes

Servings: 10 meatballs

Ingredients:

1.5lb. minced chicken
3.5oz. liquid egg whites
1 almond flour
1 green bell pepper, seeded, finely chopped
2 garlic cloves, minced

1 tablespoon dried basil
1 tablespoon onion powder
1 cup mozzarella, torn into pieces
1 jalapeno, seeded, minced
2 tablespoons butter, melted

Directions:

Preheat oven to 450F.
In a bowl, combine all the ingredients.
Mix with clean hands and shape mixture into 10 meatballs.
Grease baking sheet with melted butter, and arrange the meatballs onto baking sheet.
Bake the meatballs for 10-12 minutes or until golden brown.
Serve immediately.

Nutritional Info: Per serving/meatball

Calories: 142

Cholesterol: 60mg

Protein: 11.8g

Total fat: 4.9

Total Carbs: 1.3g

Lettuce Turkey Fajita Wrap

Preparation Time: 5 minutes
Cooking Time: 10 minutes

Servings: 4 wraps

Ingredients:

1.25lb. ground turkey
2 tablespoons butter
1 red bell pepper, seeded, sliced
2 garlic cloves, minced
5oz. mushrooms
½ tablespoon olive oil

1 teaspoon dried oregano
¼ teaspoon salt
¼ teaspoon cumin powder
¼ teaspoon black pepper
4 leaves lettuce

Directions:

Heat large pan with butter over medium-high heat.

Add the turkey and cook until browned, for 6 minutes. Remove from the pan and place aside.

Heat remaining oil and toss in the onion, mushrooms and bell pepper. Cook until tender for 5 minutes.

Add the garlic, oregano, and cumin. Cook for 1 minute.

Add back turkey and season with salt and pepper.

Cook all together for 1 minute. Divide the turkey between four lettuce leaves and wrap.

Serve after.

Nutritional Info: Per serving

Calories: 357

Cholesterol: 160mg

Protein: 29.3g

Total fat: 23.3g

Total Carbs: 3.3g

FRESH MEDITERRANEAN KEBABS

Preparation Time: 5 minutes

Cooking Time: 10 minutes

Servings: 4 kebabs

Ingredients:

1lb. beef tenderloin, cubed

½ lb. button mushrooms, stems removed

2 garlic cloves, finely chopped

1 teaspoon fresh chopped mint

1 teaspoon dried thyme

1 teaspoon dried basil

½ teaspoon smoked paprika

2 tablespoons lime juice

2 tablespoons fresh parsley, chopped

1 tablespoon melted ghee

1 teaspoon lime zest

¼ teaspoon salt

¼ teaspoon cayenne pepper

Directions:

In a mini blender, combine the garlic, mint, thyme, basil, paprika, lime juice, parsley, ghee, lime zest, and cayenne pepper. Process until smooth.

Arrange the beef tenderloin and mushrooms onto skewers and season with salt. Preheat the grill to medium-high.

Brush the skewers with prepared herb mix. Grill the skewers for 4 minutes per side, brushing after each minute.

Serve while still hot.

Nutritional Info: Per serving

Calories: 251

Cholesterol: 104mg

Protein: 34.9g

Total fat: 10.6g

Total Carbs: 3.0g

SWEET AND SOUR CHICKEN WITH CAULIFLOWER RICE

Preparation Time: 5 minutes
Cooking Time: 15 minutes   Servings: 4

Ingredients:

1 ½ lb. chicken breasts, cut into cubes
2 teaspoons garlic powder
½ cup chicken stock
¼ cup Eyrthritol
1 tablespoon coconut BCAA (amino acids)

½ cup white vinegar
½ medium head cauliflower
½ teaspoon black pepper
1 teaspoon arrowroot powder

Directions:

Cut the cauliflower into florets. Place in a food blender and process until resembles the rice. Place aside. Heat some oil in large pan. Season the chicken with garlic powder and black pepper. Cook for 4-5 minutes. Toss in the cauliflower and cook until done. Just a few minutes. Meanwhile, in a saucepan combine the chicken stock, Erythritol, coconut aminos, vinegar and arrowroot. Bring to boil. Reduce heat and simmer for 2 minutes or until slightly thickened. Pour over chicken and cauliflower.
Give it all a good stir and serve while still hot.

Nutritional Info: Per serving

Calories: 336
Total fat: 12.7g

Cholesterol: 151mg
Total Carbs: 1.6g

Protein: 39.6g

ASIAN STYLE TUNA BALLS

Preparation Time: 10 minutes
Cooking Time: 6 minutes   Servings: 12 balls

Ingredients:

10oz. can water-packed tuna
1 medium potato, cooked and mashed
1 medium egg
2 spring onions, chopped finely
3 tablespoons lime juice
1 tablespoon fish sauce

2 tablespoons coconut aminos
1 tablespoon minced ginger
2 tablespoons sesame seeds
1 red chili pepper, seeded, minced
4 tablespoons ghee

Directions:

Flake the tuna in a bowl. Add the remaining ingredients, except the sesame seeds, and mix with clean hands until blended. Shape the prepared mixture into 12 balls.
Heat ghee in a non-stick pan. Fry the tuna balls for 5-6 minutes or until golden and nice outer crust is formed. Sprinkle immediately with sesame seeds and serve.

Nutritional Info: Per serving/meatball

Calories: 122
Total fat: 7.2g

Cholesterol: 32mg
Total Carbs: 3.1g

Protein: 7.5g

TURKEY STEAKS

Preparation Time: 5 minutes
Cooking Time: 15 minutes   Servings: 4 steaks

Ingredients:

1.25lb.turkey steaks, cut into four steaks
¼ teaspoon dried thyme
¼ teaspoon dried oregano
½ teaspoon garlic powder

½ teaspoon paprika
½ teaspoon onion powder
¼ teaspoon cayenne pepper
4 tablespoons butter

Directions:

Combine the spices and herbs bowl.
Rub the turkey steaks with prepared spic mix.
Heat butter in a skillet over medium-high heat. Add the turkey steaks and cook for 5-6 minutes per side or until cooked through and the juices run clear.
Serve the turkey steaks while hot.

Nutritional Info: Per serving

Calories: 347   Cholesterol: 138mg   Protein: 31.8g
Total fat: 18.7g   Total Carbs: 0.8g

CHICKEN SATAY

Preparation Time: 10 minutes
Cooking Time: 10 minutes   Servings: 4

Ingredients:

1lb. chicken
3 teaspoons lime juice
1 red chili pepper, seeded and chopped
2 teaspoons coconut aminos
2 teaspoons organic peanut butter
2 tablespoons unsalted butter, softened

6 spring onions, chopped
1 teaspoon ginger
6 stalks coriander, chopped
¼ cup water
2 garlic cloves
1 pinch black pepper

Directions:

In a food blender, combine the lime juice, chili pepper, coconut aminos, butter, peanut butter, coriander, water, and garlic. Pulse until smooth. Slice the chicken and pour over half the prepared mixture.
Meanwhile, heat some coconut oil in a pan. Cook the spring onions and ginger for few minutes. Remove from the pan. Remove the chicken breasts from the marinade and cook for 4 minutes per side.
Stir in the ginger and onions and toss gently.
Serve the chicken with remaining marinade, sprinkled with onions and ginger.

Nutritional Info: Per serving

Calories: 249   Cholesterol: 308mg   Protein: 34.1g
Total fat: 10.6g   Total Carbs: 3.1g

SPICY AND FRUITY BURGERS

Preparation Time: 5 minutes
Cooking Time: 15 minutes   Servings: 6 burger

Ingredients:

1.5lb. minced beef
2 medium eggs
1oz. liquid egg white
1.5oz. sultanas, chopped
½ cup coconut flour
4 spring onions, chopped
½ teaspoon ground powdered ginger

½ teaspoon ground coriander seeds
¼ teaspoon ground white pepper
¼ teaspoon turmeric
¼ teaspoon all spice
½ teaspoon salt
1 pinch cinnamon

Directions:

Preheat grill to medium-high. In a bowl, combine all the ingredients. Mix with clean hands. Shape the mixture into six burgers. Grill the burgers for 15 minutes in total.
Serve after with low-carb toasted buns.

Nutritional Info: Per serving/burger

Calories: 243   Cholesterol: 156mg   Protein: 32.7g
Total fat: 8.6g   Total Carbs: 2.3g

MEXICAN CHICKEN STEAK WITH CAULIFLOWER

Preparation Time: 5 minutes
Cooking Time: 15 minutes   Servings: 4

Ingredients:

1.5lb. chicken steak, cut into strips
3 tablespoons butter
1 green bell pepper, seeded, sliced
1 tablespoon tomato puree

½ bouillon cube, crumbled
5oz. cauliflower florets
2 tablespoon Cajun seasoning

Directions:

Bring the small pot of water to boil over medium-high heat. Place in the stock cube and add the cauliflower florets. Boil for 5 minutes.
Meanwhile, heat the olive oil in a large pan. Cook the bell peppers for 5 minutes or until tender.
Remove the peppers from the pan. Add the chicken strips and cook until no longer pink.
Place back the peppers and mix with the chicken.
Add the Cajun seasoning and give it all a good stir. Toss in the cauliflower.
Cook, for 1 minute. Serve after.

Nutritional Info: Per serving

Calories: 353   Cholesterol: 154mg   Protein: 40.5g
Total fat: 13.9g   Total Carbs: 4.2g

RED CHICKEN SALAD

Preparation time: 10 minutes   Servings: 2

Ingredients:

6oz. grilled chicken meat, sliced
2 cups arugula
¼ cup pumpkin seeds

For the dressing:

1 garlic clove, minced

2 tablespoons lemon juice
¼ teaspoon salt
1 pinch ground pepper
1 tablespoon raw cider vinegar
1 teaspoon tomato paste
1 teaspoon mustard

Directions:

Prepare the dressing: in a mini blender combine all the dressing ingredients. Blend until smooth.
Prepare the salad: toss the grilled chicken, arugula, pumpkin seeds, and tomatoes in a bowl.
Pour over prepared dressing and toss gently. Serve immediately

Nutritional Info: Per serving

Calories: 617   Cholesterol: 225mg   Protein: 43.2g
Total fat: 28.5g   Total Carbs: 5.8g

A DAY AHEAD PORK AND APPLES

Preparation Time: 2 minutes
Cooking Time: 18 minutes   Servings: 4

Ingredients:

4 5oz. pork loin steaks
½ cup apple cider vinegar
2 tablespoons coconut oil
2 tablespoons coconut aminos
1 red apple, cored and sliced
¼ cup Balsamic vinegar

½ teaspoon paprika
½ teaspoon cayenne pepper
1 garlic clove, minced
¼ teaspoon salt
¼ teaspoon pepper

Directions:

*A day ahead: in a bowl, combine the cider vinegar, 1 ½ tablespoons olive oil, coconut aminos, paprika, cayenne pepper, garlic, salt, and pepper. Add the pork and cover. Refrigerate overnight.
The next day: hate the remaining olive oil in a pan. Add apple and cook for 6-7 minutes or until tender. Stir in the balsamic vinegar and cook until evaporated.
Meanwhile, remove the pork from the marinade. Discard the marinade. Preheat the grill.
Grill the pork until the inner temperature reaches 145F/62C.
Serve grilled steaks with onions and apple on top. Enjoy.

Nutritional Info: Per serving

Calories: 443   Cholesterol: 113mg   Protein: 29.9g
Total fat: 26.7g   Total Carbs: 8.7g

Steak Salad with Raspberries

Preparation Time: 10 minutes
Cooking Time: 10 minutes   Servings: 4

Ingredients:

1lb. sirloin steak
½ cup raspberries
8 cups baby spinach
3 tablespoons raspberry vinegar
1 tablespoon minced shallot

½ cup crushed almonds
1oz. crumbled feta
2 tablespoons butter, melted
½ teaspoon salt, divided

Directions:

Place ¼ cup raspberries, raspberry vinegar, shallot, ¼ teaspoon salt and ¼ cup almonds in the food blender. Pulse until you have a paste. While the blender is running low, add the melted butter and pulse until smooth. Place aside.

Preheat the grill. Season the steak with remaining salt.

Grill the steak for 5 minutes per side for medium-rare. Let the steak rest for 5 minutes before slicing into strips.

In a bowl, combine the spinach with remaining raspberries, almonds and crumbled feta. Add the steak and drizzle all with prepared raspberry vinaigrette.

Gently toss and serve.

Nutritional Info: Per serving

Calories: 306
Total fat: 14.7g

Cholesterol: 123mg
Total Carbs: 4.8g

Protein: 27.4g

Coconut Shrimps with sauce

Preparation Time: 5 minutes
Cooking Time: 10 minutes   Servings: 4

Ingredients:

1lb. shrimps, peeled and deveined
1 large egg
¾ cup coconut flour
¼ teaspoon salt
¼ teaspoon black pepper

For the sauce:

1 tablespoon fish sauce
1 tablespoon Sriracha or some other hot sauce
2 tablespoons chopped coriander
4 tablespoons heavy cream
1 red chili pepper, seeded, minced

Directions:

Prepare the sauce: in a food blender, combine all the sauce ingredients.

Pulse until blended and smooth. Place aside.

Prepare the shrimps: rinse the peeled and deveined shrimps. Gently pat dry with kitchen towels.

Whisk the egg in a bowl. place the coconut flour, salt, and pepper in a separate bowl.
Heat some coconut oil in a frying pan.
Dip the shrimps into egg and dredge through the seasoned coconut flour.
Fry the shrimps for 45-50 seconds and place onto a paper towel lined plate.
Repeat with remaining shrimps. Serve shrimps while still hot with prepared sauce.

Nutritional Info: Per serving

Calories: 211   Cholesterol: 306mg   Protein: 28.0g
Total fat: 8.7g   Total Carbs: 3.3g

BEEF SIRLOIN SKEWERS

Preparation Time: 10 minutes
Cooking Time: 7 minutes   Servings: 16 skewers

Ingredients:

2lb. sirloin steak, cut into bite-size pieces   2 teaspoons salt
¼ cup melted butter   1 ½ tablespoons ground cumin seeds
4 medium peaches, cut into wedges   1 tablespoon cracked black pepper
2 green bell pepper, cut into 16 pieces

Directions:

In a bowl, combine steak, with peaches, , red bell pepper, green bell pepper, salt, cumin, butter, and black pepper. Toss gently to coat.
Thread steak, onion, peaches, green and red bell pepper onto skewers. Alternate the ingredients.
Preheat the grill. Grill the skewers for 6-7 minutes, turning occasionally.
Serve warm.

Nutritional Info: Per serving/skewer

Calories: 151   Cholesterol: 58mg   Protein: 17.8g
Total fat: 6.6g   Total Carbs: 3.9g

FAST ASIAN STYLE FLOUNDER FILLETS

Preparation Time: 5 minutes
Cooking Time: 10 minutes   Servings: 4 fillets

Ingredients:

4 4oz. flounder fillets or cod fillets   ½ cup chopped coriander
1 tablespoon minced ginger root   2 tablespoons coconut oil
2 teaspoons rice vinegar   ¼ teaspoon salt
2 teaspoons coconut amino acids (BCAAs)

Directions:

Season the fish fillets with salt.
Heat oil in the pan. Add the ginger, rice vinegar and cook for 2-3 minutes. Remove from the pan.

Place the flounder in the same pan and cook for 3-5 minutes or until lightly brown.
Drizzle the flounder with coconut aminos and top with ginger and chopped coriander.
Toss in the pan gently and cover. Let the flavors combine for 5 minutes.
Serve after.

Nutritional Info: Per serving/skewer

Calories: 194

Total fat: 8.6g

Cholesterol: 77mg

Total Carbs: 0.2g

Protein: 27.5g

Chicken Mushroom Stir-Fry

Preparation Time: 5 minutes

Cooking Time: 10 minutes

Servings: 4

Ingredients:

1lb. chicken breast fillets, thinly sliced
7oz. spiralized zucchini spaghetti
7oz. green beans, trimmed and cut into small pieces
5oz. white mushrooms, sliced

2 tablespoons olive oil
3 tablespoons coconut aminos
1-inch ginger, peeled, chopped
1 bunch Chinese broccoli, stalks and leaves separated, sliced

Directions:

Place the zucchinis in a bowl. Cover with boiling water and soak for 5 minutes.
Heat 1 teaspoon oil in a frying pan. Add chicken and cook for 3 minutes or until golden. Place aside.
Add remaining oil and stir-fry ginger for 1-2 minutes. Add mushrooms and stir-fry for 1 minute.
Add the beans and broccoli and stir-fry for 2 minutes.
Return chicken to the pan. Add zucchinis, and coconut aminos.
Toss for 1 minute until everything is coated.
Serve after and enjoy.

Nutritional Info: Per serving

Calories: 298

Total fat: 15.6g

Cholesterol: 101mg

Total Carbs: 4.7g

Protein: 34.8g

Keto Fast Salad

Preparation time: 5 minutes

Cooking time: 10 minutes

Servings: 2

Ingredients:

4oz. ham
1oz. blue cheese
2 eggs, hard-boiled
¼ avocado, sliced
2 cups lettuce

For the dressing:

1 teaspoon mustard
1 teaspoon lemon juice
3 tablespoon olive oil
1 tablespoon apple cider vinegar, organic
Salt and pepper - to taste

Directions:

Chop the ham in cubes and cook in non-stick skillet, with few drops of oil for 3-5 minutes.

Meanwhile, slice the eggs and torn salad in bite size pieces. Place the salad in a bowl and top with blue cheese, avocado and eggs. Add cooked ham and place aside.

Whisk the dressing ingredients and pour over salad, toss to combine and serve.

Nutritional Info: Per serving

Calories: 454

Total fat: 39.8g

Cholesterol: 207mg

Total Carbs: 7.4g

Protein: 19.1g

CHORIZO SALAD

Preparation time: 5 minutes   Cooking time: 4 minutes   Servings: 4

Ingredients:

4 oz. radicchio, torn into pieces or arugula
4 oz. escarole
1 cup sliced Picante Chorizo sausage
1 garlic clove, minced
3 tablespoons extra virgin olive oil

½ cup thinly sliced celery hearts
½ tablespoon finely grated lemon zest
2 tablespoons lemon juice
Fresh round salt and pepper

Directions:

Heat some oil in a large skillet and fry chorizo until nicely browned.

Meanwhile in a large bowl combine all remaining ingredients and when chorizo is fried add as well, toss to combine. Serve in a small bowls.

Nutritional Info: Per serving

Calories: 244

Total fat: 22.3g

Cholesterol: 26mg

Total Carbs: 3.5g

Protein: 8.5g

ZUCCHINI-RASPBERRY SALAD

Preparation time: 15 minutes   Servings: 2

Ingredients:

2 cups zucchini, spirals
2 tablespoons pistachios, shelled and crushed
2 tablespoons goat cheese, crumbled
1 teaspoon basil, dried and crushed

For the dressing:

4 tablespoons olive oil
¼ cup raspberries
4 tablespoons balsamic vinegar
¼ teaspoon garlic, minced
Salt and pepper – to taste

Directions:

Combine spiral zucchinis, pistachios, goat cheese, and basil in a bowl.

In a mini food blender combine the dressing ingredients, pulse until blended through.

Pour the dressing over salad, toss to combine and serve.

Nutritional Info: Per serving

Calories: 293

Total fat: 30.1g

Cholesterol: 0mg

Total Carbs: 7.0g

Protein: 2.3g

CHICKEN AND BLACKBERRY SALAD

Preparation time: 15 minutes   Servings: 2

Ingredients:

14oz. chicken breasts, grilled and shredded (you can also use leftovers)

½ cup artichoke hearts, canned, rinsed, drained and sliced

1.5oz. black olives, pitted

2oz. blackberries

1 tablespoon blackberry vinegar

7oz. lettuce

2 tablespoon extra-virgin olive oil

Directions:

Wash lettuce and place aside to dry, torn into bite size pieces and place in a bowl.

Drain and slice the artichoke hearts and spread over salad, followed by shredded chicken. Add olives and raspberries. Drizzle all with blackberry vinegar and extra-virgin olive oil, toss to combine and serve.

Nutritional Info: Per serving

Calories: 547

Total fat: 31.3g

Cholesterol: 177mg

Total Carbs: 7.0g

Protein: 48.4g

SPICY CHICKEN WINGS

Preparation time: 5 minutes   Cooking time: 30 minutes   Servings: 6

Ingredients:

2lb. chicken wings

2 tablespoons poultry seasoning

½ cup sugar-free syrup

2 tablespoons water

1 tablespoon hot sauce

1 ½ teaspoons garlic, chopped

Salt and pepper – to taste

Directions:

Combine syrup, water, poultry seasoning and chopped garlic in large sauce pan. Bring to boil over medium-high heat. Add wings to the pot and reduce heat simmer, covered for 5 minutes. Uncover wings and simmer for 20 minutes more. Transfer wings onto wide plate and continue simmering sauce for 5 minutes or until slightly thickens. Season sauce with salt and pepper, add hot sauce and return wings to the pot, stir to coat well. Meanwhile, preheat broiler.

Arrange wings onto broiler pan and cook for 5 minutes per side or until crispy. Serve while still hot.

NOTE: Hot sauce contains chili and is well known that chili acts like metabolism booster.

Nutritional Info: Per serving

Calories: 302

Total fat: 11.3g

Cholesterol: 135mg

Total Carbs: 3.8g

Protein: 43.9g

BACON WITH VEAL LIVER AND PEPPERCORNS

Preparation time: 5 minutes   Cooking time: 10 minutes   Servings: 4

Ingredients:

8 pieces bacon
1 ¼ lb. veal liver, cut into slices

2 tablespoons green peppercorns, whole
2 tablespoons butter

Directions:

Heat non-stick skillet over medium high heat.

Add bacon and cook until crispy. Place on paper towels to drain and crumble.

Heat butter in a skillet. Add liver slices and cook for 2 minutes per side. Transfer liver onto serving platter.

Place peppercorns into heated skillet just until warmed through.

Spoon over liver and add crumbled bacon. Serve while still hot.

Nutritional Info: Per serving

Calories: 376   Cholesterol: 469mg   Protein: 32.7g
Total fat: 17.8g   Total Carbs: 8.6g

KETO CHILI

Preparation time: 15 minutes   Cooking time: 50 minutes   Servings: 4

Ingredients:

1lb. beef, minced
1lb. sirloin steaks, diced in 1-inch pieces
2 tablespoons fish sauce
Salt and pepper - to taste
1 teaspoon smoked paprika
1 ¼ teaspoon cumin, ground
1 teaspoon oregano or basil, dried

2 tablespoons coconut aminos
1 tablespoon chili powder
¼ teaspoon cayenne pepper

4 garlic cloves, minced
3 tablespoons ghee
1 ¼ cup beef broth

Directions:

Grease pan with ghee and heat over medium-high heat, add garlic and cook for 1-2 minutes, stirring.

Add sirloin and minced beef and cook until browned on all sides.

Combine all dry spices in small bowl, cumin, paprika, chili powder, cayenne, salt, pepper, and oregano. Sprinkle the spices over meat.

Stir in beef broth, coconut aminos and fish sauce, reduce heat to medium, cover and simmer for 50 minutes. Serve warm.

Nutritional Info: Per serving

Calories: 536
Total fat: 24.7g
Cholesterol: 227mg
Total Carbs: 3.5g
Protein: 43.1g

BEEF DANISH MEATBALLS

Preparation time: 15 minutes   Cooking time: 20 minutes   Servings: 6

Ingredients:

1lb. beef, ground
1 egg
1 cup ricotta cheese
1 ½ teaspoons allspice
Pinch of black pepper

1 ½ teaspoons nutmeg
4oz. Swiss cheese
1 tablespoon butter
1 ½ teaspoons salt

Directions:

Melt butter in skillet over medium-high heat, add onions and cook until tender. Remove from the heat and cool for 10 minutes.

Shred the Swiss cheese and place in food processor, process until you get a fine crumble. Place aside.

In a mixing bowl, combine egg with ricotta cheese. Stir in spices and mix until blended thoroughly. Stir in onions and cheese and finally add beef. Mix until ingredients come together.

Preheat oven to 350F and line baking sheet with parchment paper. Form 30 meat balls from the mixture and place onto baking sheet. Bake the meatballs for 20 minutes, serve after with fresh salad

Nutritional Info: Per serving

Calories: 301
Total fat: 16.1g

Cholesterol: 130mg
Total Carbs: 3.8g

Protein: 33.7g

COCONUT SHRIMPS

Preparation time: 5 minutes   Cooking time: 10 minutes   Servings: 4

Ingredients:

1lb. shrimps, deveined
¾ cup coconut, unsweetened and shredded finely
2 tablespoons vegetable oil – to fry
1 egg, whisked
¾ teaspoon salt
1 pinch black pepper

2 teaspoons water

Directions:

Peel and devein the shrimps. Place aside in clean bowl and cover.

Beat the egg in small bowl with water until slightly frothy.

In separate bowl combine together coconut, salt and pepper.

Preheat large non-stick skillet over medium-high heat, add 1 tablespoon oil.

While oil is heating up, dip shrimps in egg and in coconut mixture, one at the time.

Fill the pan with half of the shrimps, cook shrimps for 3 minutes per side.

Transfer shrimps onto plate, lined with kitchen paper to drain, and heat up remaining oil before cooking remaining shrimps. Serve while still hot.

Nutritional Info: Per serving

Calories: 190.4

Total fat: 8.2g

Cholesterol: 217.5mg

Total carbohydrate: 3.4g

Protein: 24.9g

GRILLED RED SNAPPER

Preparation time: 5 minutes

Cooking time: 15 minutes

Servings: 4

Ingredients:

1lb. red snapper fillets

4 tablespoon extra-virgin olive oil

¼ cup white wine, dry

1 tablespoon parsley, fresh, chopped

1 tablespoon basil, fresh, chopped

1 ½ tablespoons lemon juice

½ teaspoon chili powder

Salt and pepper – to taste

4 tablespoons chive, chopped

1/3 lemon, cut into slices

Directions:

Prepare the marinade, in a medium bowl whisk together olive oil, chili powder, pepper, salt, lemon juice, salt, wine, parsley and basil.

Prepare the fish, place red snapper fillets in a baking pan and pour over marinade.

Place lemon slices all over fish and cover with clean foil.

Refrigerate fish for 1 hour. Preheat grill and coat grill rack with cooking spray.

Remove fish from marinade and place onto grill rack.

Cook fish for 15 minutes, covered with aluminum foil. Fish is done when flakes easily.

Serve while still hot, garnished with chives.

Nutritional Info: Per serving

Calories: 281

Total fat: 16.1g

Cholesterol: 53mg

Total Carbs: 0.9g

Protein: 30.1g

SALMON STUFFED AVOCADO

Preparation time: 5 minutes

Cooking time: 25 minutes

Servings: 4

Ingredients:

2 small avocados

4 tablespoons lemon juice

2 tablespoons ghee, melted

14oz. salmon fillets

4oz. crème fraiche

Salt and pepper – to taste

Directions:

Preheat oven to 400F and place salmon fillets on baking tray lined with parchment paper.

Drizzle the fillets with melted ghee and season to taste. Drizzle with 2 tablespoons lemon juice.

Bake salmon for 25 minutes or until flakes easily. Place aside to cool and flake salmon using fork. Transfer in a bowl and add sour crème and remaining lemon juice. Scoop the avocado flesh, leaving nice ½-inch thick shell and cut the cooped flesh into small pieces, combine with salmon and fill the avocado shells with prepared mix. Sprinkle with some dill before serving.

Nutritional Info: Per serving

Calories: 449

Total fat: 37.5g

Cholesterol: 71mg

Total Carbs: 10.0g

Protein: 22.1g

CAULIFLOWER AND TURNIP SOUP

Preparation time: 5 minutes   Cooking time: 20 minutes   Servings: 4

Ingredients:

1.5lb. cauliflower
5oz. turnip, peeled and diced
2 cups chicken stock
Salt – to taste

4 tablespoons ghee
5oz. chorizo, chopped

Directions:

Wash the cauliflower and cut into small florets, set aside.
Melt 2 tablespoons ghee in Dutch oven and add prepared cauliflower and cook for 5-6 minutes, stirring.
Stir in chicken stock and cover with lid, cook for 10 minutes.
Meanwhile, melt the remaining ghee and cook chorizo with turnips for 8-10 minutes.
Transfer half of the chorizo mixture into soup, remove soup from the heat and blend using immersion blender. Season to taste, serve in small bowls and top with reserved chorizo mix.

Nutritional Info: Per serving

Calories: 335

Total fat: 26.8g

Cholesterol: 64mg

Total Carbs: 10.0g

Protein: 12.3g

SUPER SOUP

Preparation time: 10 minutes   Cooking time: 10 minutes   Servings: 6

Ingredients:

14oz. cauliflower head, cut into florets
5oz. watercress
7oz. spinach, thawed
4 cups chicken stock

1 cup heavy cream
¼ cup ghee
Salt and pepper – to taste
2 garlic cloves, crushed

Directions:

Grease Dutch oven with ghee, place over medium-high heat and add garlic. Cook until browned and stir cauliflower florets. Cook for 5 minutes. Add spinach and water cress and cook for 2 minutes or until just wilted, pour in vegetable stock and bring to boil. Cook until cauliflower is crisp-tender and stir in the heavy cream. Season with salt and pepper and remove from the heat, process the soup using immersion blender until creamy. Serve immediately.

Nutritional Info: Per serving

Calories: 188

Total fat: 16.6g

Cholesterol: 49mg

Total Carbs: 7.9g

Protein: 4.1g

JALAPENO SOUP

Preparation time: 5 minutes   Cooking time: 15 minutes   Servings: 4

Ingredients:

4 jalapeno peppers
4 slices bacon, raw
2 tablespoons salsa
2 cups chicken stock

½ teaspoon garlic powder
4oz. cream cheese
½ cup heavy cream
1 cup Monterey Jack cheese, shredded

Directions:

Cook the bacon in non-stick skillet until crisp, remove, chop and place aside on paper towel.

In same pan add heavy cream, cream cheese and chicken stock, bring to simmer over medium heat and cook for few minutes, stirring.

Whisk in salsa Verde, chili powder and shredded cheese. Continue cooking until cheese is melted.

Meanwhile, wash the jalapenos until charred and soft, peel the skin, remove seeds and chop finely. Add to soup and cook for 5 minutes.

Season with salt and pepper and continue cooking until soup is thickened slightly. Remove from heat, serve in bowls and top with chopped bacon before serving.

Nutritional Info: Per serving

Calories: 304   Cholesterol: 84mg   Protein: 12.4g
Total fat: 27.1g   Total Carbs: 3.6g

KETO SPINACH BISQUE

Preparation time: 5 minutes   Cooking time: 30 minutes   Servings: 4

Ingredients:

28oz. spinach
1 cup heavy cream
1 teaspoon fresh ground pepper
4 cups chicken stock
½ cup grated Parmesan

1 bunch celery, chopped
½ cup basil, chopped
2 tablespoon olive oil
Salt and pepper – to taste

Directions:

Heat olive oil in large pot over medium-high heat, add celery and cook until tender.

Pour chicken stock and spinach in the pot, bring mixture to simmer and season with salt and pepper. Simmer for 30 minutes.

Turn off heat and using immersion blender puree until smooth.

Stir in heavy cream, basil and Parmesan cheese.

Serve immediately.

Nutritional Info: Per serving

Calories: 269   Cholesterol: 52mg   Protein: 11.9g
Total fat: 22.7g   Total Carbs: 9.7g

SWEET-PEA WARM SALAD

Preparation time: 5 minutes   Cooking time: 15 minutes   Servings: 4

Ingredients:

6oz.snap pea, chopped into 5 slices per pod
1 tablespoon rosemary, fresh
4 tablespoon butter

1 tablespoon coconut oil
½ cup shredded coconut, unsweetened
Salt and pepper – to taste

Directions:

Melt butter in skillet over medium-high heat. Add coconut oil and stir, add shredded coconut and stir until fully coated.
Add rosemary and stir until combined, lower heat to low and cook the coconut, stirring for 10 minutes.
Add the chopped pea pods and mix to combine. Cook for 5 minutes and serve warm.

Nutritional Info: Per serving

Calories: 204   Cholesterol: 31mg   Protein: 2.8g
Total fat: 18.6g   Total Carbs: 8.2g

THAI CHICKEN SALAD

Preparation time: 5 minutes + inactive time   Servings: 4
Cooking time: 10 minutes

Ingredients:

1lb. chicken breasts, sliced into ¼-inch thick stripes
1 zucchini, sliced thinly into strips
1 ½ teaspoons curry paste, mild
3 tablespoons lime juice
2 garlic cloves, crushed
Salt and pepper – to taste

For the dressing:
2 teaspoons agave syrup
4 tablespoons extra-virgin olive oil
2 tablespoons lime juice
1 tablespoon fish sauce
1 tablespoon chopped cilantro
2 garlic cloves, minced

Directions:

Combine curry paste, lime juice and garlic, season with salt and pepper. Place the chicken strips into bow and pour over curry paste, cover and marinate for 30 minutes.
After 30 minutes, remove chicken from marinade and grill on high for 5-6 minutes per side.
While the chicken is cooking prepare the dressing, in a food blender combine all dressing ingredients.
Combine prepared veggies with chicken and pour over prepared dressing. Toss to combine and serve.

Nutritional Info: Per serving

Calories: 382   Cholesterol: 101mg   Protein: 23.9g
Total fat: 23.6g   Total Carbs: 6.1g

TUNA SALAD

Preparation time: 5 minutes   Cooking time: 10 minutes   Servings: 4

Ingredients:

2 cups lettuce
½ avocado, sliced
7oz. tuna, can
1 tablespoon balsamic vinegar
¼ cup min, fresh, chopped

½ cup olives, pitted and chopped
½ cup parsley, chopped
4 tablespoons extra-virgin olive oil
2 zucchinis, small, sliced thinly
Salt and pepper – to taste

Directions:

Grill the zucchinis in grill pan until for few seconds per side. Remove from the pan, allow to cool ad cut into bite size pieces.
Add remaining ingredients and toss to combine.
Serve after.

Nutritional Info: Per serving

Calories: 255   Cholesterol: 15mg   Protein: 14.8g
Total fat: 20.1g   Total Carbs: 5.7g

STUFFED MEATLOAF

Preparation time: 5 minutes   Cooking time: 60 minutes   Servings: 4

Ingredients:

1lb. beef, ground
3 garlic cloves, minced
2 tablespoons tomato paste
2 eggs, whole
4oz. goat cheese

Handful of spinach
Salt and pepper – to taste
2 teaspoons basil, dried
½ tablespoon rosemary, fresh, chopped

Directions:

Preheat oven to 425F.
Combine meat with eggs and garlic in a bowl. Add salt, pepper, basil and rosemary and mix until blended thoroughly.
Place the meat onto piece of plastic wrap and cover with other plastic wrap, flatten the meat to ¼-inch thick rectangle. Place the cheese and spinach on one shorter end and roll the meat using plastic foil.
Transfer the prepared meatloaf into baking dish and cover with tomato puree.
Cook for 55-60 minutes and remove from the oven, cover with foil and let the meatloaf rest for 10 minutes, serve after.

Nutritional Info: Per serving

Calories: 382   Cholesterol: 213mg   Protein: 30.6g
Total fat: 19.5g   Total Carbs: 3.3g

CREAMY STEAK

Preparation time: 5 minutes   Cooking time: 10 minutes   Servings: 4

Ingredients:

4 slices Swiss cheese
1lb. steak
1 tablespoon mustard
2 tablespoon ghee

¼ cup green pepper, chopped
2 tablespoons mayonnaise
1 tablespoon olive oil
1 tablespoon garlic, minced

Directions:

Melt ghee over medium-low heat in a frying pan. Add in garlic, and pepper. Cook until tender, stirring for 5-6 minutes.
Add olive oil and shaved steak, cook the steak all the way through for 7-8 minutes.
Turn the heat to low and add mayonnaise and mustard, stir well and top the meat with cheese slices. Allow to stand for 1 minute or until melted.
Mix once again and serve after.

Nutritional Info: Per serving

Calories: 464   Cholesterol: 146mg   Protein: 30.9g
Total fat: 26.6g   Total Carbs: 5.2g

EASY TACO PIE

Preparation time: 5 minutes   Cooking time: 30 minutes   Servings: 8

Ingredients:

1 lb. beef, ground
4 eggs
2 garlic cloves, minced
Salt and pepper – to taste

1 cup heavy cream
1 cup Cheddar cheese, shredded
¾ cup water
3 tablespoon taco seasoning

Directions:

Preheat oven to 350F and grease 9-inch baking ceramic pan.
Brown beef in large skillet over medium-high heat. Add taco seasoning and stir, add water and reduce heat to medium-low. Cook for few minutes until sauce is thickened.
Spread beef in prepared pan and place aside. Whisk eggs with cream, salt, pepper and garlic. Pour over beef and top with cheese, bake for 30 minutes or until center is set. Serve topped with tomato or avocado.

Nutritional Info: Per serving

Calories: 247   Cholesterol: 168mg   Protein: 23.8g
Total fat: 16.9g   Total Carbs: 1.0g

CREAMY SHRIMPS WITH BACON

Preparation time: 5 minutes   Cooking time: 10 minutes   Servings: 4

Ingredients:

4oz. smoked salmon
6oz. shrimps, deveined
½ cup heavy cream
4 slices bacon, cut into 1-inch pieces

½ cup mushrooms, sliced
1 tablespoon ghee
Salt and pepper – to taste

Directions:

Heat non-stick skillet over medium heat, add bacon and cook until juts crispy. Add ghee and melt.
Add mushrooms and cook for 5 minutes. Slice salmon into strips and add to mushrooms, cook for 2-3 minutes.
Ad shrimps, increase heat to high and cook for 2 minutes, stir in cream, season to taste and cook for 1 minute. Serve immediately.

Nutritional Info: Per serving

Calories: 200   Cholesterol: 132mg   Protein: 17.8g
Total fat: 14.3g   Total Carbs: 1.5g

BACON WRAPPED SCALLOPS

Preparation time: 5 minutes   Cooking time: 5 minutes   Servings: 4

Ingredients:

1 tablespoon vegetable oil
12 scallops

12 bacon slices
Salt and pepper – to taste

Directions:

Wash and pat dry scallops.
Wrap each bacon slice around scallop and secure with toothpick. Season with salt and pepper.
Heat vegetable oil in large skillet over medium heat, place wrapped scallops into heated oil and cook 2 ½ minutes per side. Serve immediately.

Nutritional Info: Per serving

Calories: 418   Cholesterol: 92mg   Protein: 26.2g
Total fat: 27.9g   Total Carbs: 2.9g

BAKED SALMON IN FOIL

Preparation time: 5 minutes   Cooking time: 15 minutes   Servings: 4

Ingredients:

1lb. salmon
4 tablespoons butter, cubed

¼ teaspoon Italian seasoning
2 tablespoons lemon juice

Salt and pepper – to taste
2 garlic cloves, minced

¼ teaspoon red pepper flakes

Directions:

Preheat oven to 375F and prepare baking dish.

Combine lemon juice and garlic in sauce pan, heat over medium heat allowing lemon juice to reduce to 1 tablespoon. Add in 2 tablespoons butter and remove from the heat, stir until butter melts.

Repeat with remaining butter, heating if needed.

Place the salmon onto piece of aluminum foil, large enough to close into packet. Generously season salmon with salt and pepper and pour over butter mix, sprinkle with red pepper flakes and Italian seasoning. Fold the foil to create packet and transfer salmon onto baking tray. Bake for 15 minutes. After the time has run, open the packet and broil the salmon for 2-3 minutes. Serve immediately.

Nutritional Info: Per serving

Calories: 257	Cholesterol: 81mg	Protein: 20.3g
Total fat: 19.7g	Total Carbs: 0.7g	

CHILLED AVOCADO SOUP

Preparation time: 5 minutes	Cooking time: 5 minutes	Servings: 4

Ingredients:

1 cup pureed avocado
1 ½ cup vegetable broth
1 teaspoon cumin, ground

1 jalapeno pepper, seeded and chopped
1 ½ cups heavy cream
Salt – to taste

Directions:

In a food blender combine all ingredients by order.
Pulse until smooth and blended thoroughly.
Serve immediately or you can reheat soup for few minutes over medium-high heat.

Nutritional Info: Per serving

Calories: 188	Cholesterol: 62mg	Protein: 3.1g
Total fat: 18.5g	Total Carbs: 2.8g	

MUSHROOM AND FENNEL SOUP

Preparation time: 5 minutes	Cooking time: 20 minutes	Servings: 4

Ingredients:

4 tablespoons butter
4 cups vegetable stock
1 cup leeks, sliced
15oz. heavy cream

8oz. mushrooms
1 cup fennel bulb, sliced
Salt – to taste

Directions:

Bring stock to boil over medium-high heat and continue boiling until reduced by half.

Melt butter in large sauce pot over medium heat, add mushrooms and cook until browned.

Add fennel and leeks and season to taste, cook stirring until tender.

Add cream and bring to boil, continue cooking until reduced by half, stirring constantly to avoid bubbling.

Add reduced stock and stir to combine, remove from the heat and puree using immersion blender. Serve after.

Nutritional Info: Per serving

Calories: 504	Cholesterol: 176mg	Protein: 8.6g
Total fat: 51.2g	Total Carbs: 10.0g	

ZUCCHINI SOUP

Preparation time: 5 minutes	Cooking time: 15 minutes	Servings: 4

Ingredients:

½ cup dill weed, chopped, fresh
2 tablespoons olive oil
4 cups chicken stock
1 chili pepper, small, seeded and chopped

2 zucchinis, medium, chopped in small cubes
½ cup grated parmesan
Salt and pepper – to taste

Directions:

Heat olive oil in medium sauce pan, add pepper and cook until tender.

Add chicken stock, season to taste and bring to simmer, continue simmering for 10 minutes.

Add zucchinis and simmer until is tender. Remove from heat and stir in dill weed and parmesan. Serve.

Nutritional Info: Per serving

Calories: 139	Cholesterol: 11mg	Protein: 7.1g
Total fat: 12.0g	Total Carbs: 5.2g	

BROCCOLI CHEESE SOUP

Preparation time: 5 minutes	Cooking time: 10 minutes	Servings: 4

Ingredients:

2 tablespoons butter
3 cup vegetable broth
8oz. cheddar cheese, shredded

4 cups broccoli florets
8oz. cream cheese
1 cup heavy cream

Directions:

Heat broth in sauce pot and bring to simmer, add broccoli and simmer until tender.

In separate pot heat the heavy cream, cheddar cheese and cream cheese with butter. Stir until melted and combined.

Once broccoli is tender remove half and puree remaining broccoli with immersion blender. Stir in prepared cheese mix and add removed broccoli, stir well to combine and serve after.

Nutritional Info: Per serving

Calories: 641	Cholesterol: 178mg	Protein: 25.3g
Total fat: 56.8g	Total Carbs: 9.8g	

CABBAGE CREAMY SOUP

Preparation time: 5 minutes   Cooking time: 25 minutes   Servings: 4

Ingredients:

2 cups chopped cabbage
4 cups chicken stock

1 cup heavy cream
4 slices bacon, cooked, crumbled

Directions:

Bring the chicken stock to boil over medium-high heat.
Add the cabbage.
Reduce the heat to low and simmer for 20-25 minutes or until the cabbage is tender.
Stir in the heavy cream and simmer for 5 minutes. Serve hot, topped with crumbled bacon.

Nutritional Info: Per serving

Calories: 156   Cholesterol: 48mg   Protein: 4.1g
Total fat: 14.3g   Total Carbs: 3.7g

GINGERED BEEF

Preparation time: 5 minutes   Cooking time: 20 minutes   Servings: 4

Ingredients:

2 4oz. beef ribeye steak, cut into strips
4 tablespoons bacon grease
2 garlic cloves, minced
2 teaspoons ground ginger

1 tablespoon coconut aminos
¼ cup apple cider vinegar
1 small zucchini, cubed
Salt and pepper, to taste

Directions:

Heat the bacon grease in a large skillet.
When hot, add the beef and cook until browned. Remove from the skillet.
Add the garlic and cook until fragrant. Add the ginger, coconut aminos, zucchini, cider vinegar, salt and pepper.
Bring to simmer and reduce heat. Add the beef strips and cook until the sauce is reduced.
Serve while still hot.

Nutritional Info: Per serving

Calories: 322   Cholesterol: 41mg   Protein: 4.3g
Total fat: 32.4g   Total Carbs: 2.5g

PORK STEW

Preparation time: 5 minutes   Cooking time: 20 minutes   Servings: 6

Ingredients:

4 tablespoons lard
0.75lb. cooked and shredded pork shoulder
2 teaspoons ground cumin
2 teaspoons chili powder
4 garlic cloves, minced
1 teaspoon dried basil
1 teaspoon smoked paprika

7oz. mushrooms, sliced
1 jalapeno pepper, seeded, sliced
1 green bell pepper, seeded, sliced
1 ½ cups bone broth
2 cups beef broth
¼ cup tomato paste

Directions:

Heat the lard in a pan. Add the mushrooms, jalapeno, garlic, and bell pepper into the pan. Cook until tender. Add the spices and cook for 1-2 minutes, stirring. Add the bone broth and beef broth. Bring to a boil. Add the pork, tomato paste and simmer for 20 minutes. Serve after.

Nutritional Info: Per serving

Calories: 288   Cholesterol: 59mg   Protein: 17.0g
Total fat: 21.7g   Total Carbs: 6.7g

MIXED MEATBALLS WITH CREAM

Preparation time: 10 minutes   Cooking time: 15 minutes   Servings: 15 meatballs

Ingredients:

0.5lb. ground lamb
0.5lb. ground pork
2 tablespoons chopped cilantro
4 garlic cloves, minced
2 teaspoons chopped fresh thyme
1 teaspoon ground coriander
½ teaspoon smoked paprika

Salt and pepper, to taste

For the cream:
2 tablespoons water
1 cup cream cheese, softened
2 teaspoons lemon juice
2 teaspoons cumin
Salt, to taste

Directions:

Prepare the cream: combine all the cream ingredients in a bowl. Cover and chill until ready to use.
Prepare the meatballs: heat oven to 350F and line a baking sheet with parchment paper.
In a large bowl, combine all ingredients. Mix with clean hands and shape into meatballs. Arrange the meatballs onto baking sheet. Bake the meatballs for 15-17 minutes or until the center is no longer pink. Serve meatballs while still hot with chilled yogurt.

Nutritional Info: Per serving/meatball

Calories: 107   Cholesterol: 42mg   Protein: 8.5g
Total fat: 7.1g   Total Carbs: 0.9g

BACON TURKEY PATTIES

Preparation time: 10 minutes   Cooking time: 10 minutes   Servings: 10 patties

Ingredients:

1lb. ground turkey, meat from the legs
½ cup almond meal
1 egg
½ cup Parmesan, grated
6 bacon slices, cooked and crumbled

2 garlic cloves, minced
4 tablespoons parsley, fresh, chopped
4 tablespoons lard
Salt and pepper, to taste

Directions:

Heat non-stick skillet over medium-high heat.

Add the bacon and cook until crispy. Transfer onto paper towels and crumble.

In a bowl, combine all the ingredients, except the lard. Add crumbled bacon and stir to combine.

Mix well to combine and shape the mixture into 10 patties.

Heat some oil in a skillet. Add the patties and cook until golden brown. Serve after.

Nutritional Info: Per serving/patty

Calories: 187   Cholesterol: 74mg   Protein: 16.4g
Total fat: 14.2g   Total Carbs: 1.6g

CRUNCHY PORK CHOPS

Preparation time: 5 minutes   Cooking time: 10 minutes   Servings: 6

Ingredients:

6 4oz. pork chops
¼ cup almond meal
2 teaspoons ground cumin
1 teaspoon coriander seeds, ground
4 tablespoons bacon fat
Salt and pepper

To serve with:

1 cup heavy cream
¼ cup white wine
1 bay leaf
Salt and pepper, to taste

Directions:

Season the pork chops to taste. In a shallow plate, combine the almond meal, cumin, and coriander.

Coat the pork chops with prepared mixture. Heat the coconut oil in a skillet.

When the oil is melted and hot, add the pork and cook for 5 minutes per side.

Remove the pork from the skillet. Add the wine to deglaze the pan. Simmer, scarping any remaining bits. Add the bay leaf and cook until wine is reduced. Stir in the heavy cream and bring to a gentle boil. Season to taste and serve.

Serve after with prepared pork.

Nutritional Info: Per serving

Calories: 544   Cholesterol: 133mg   Protein: 26.9g
Total fat: 45.7g   Total Carbs: 2.5g

ROASTED CHICKEN TIGHTS

Preparation time: 10 minutes + inactive time
Cooking time: 30 minutes

Servings: 4

Ingredients:

8 chicken legs, boneless
4 garlic cloves, minced
4 tablespoons bacon fat
2 lemons, sliced into thin round
2 tablespoons fresh thyme, chopped
Salt and pepper, to taste

For the dressing:

¼ cup sour cream
¼ cup heavy cream
2 spring onions, chopped
½ cup mayonnaise
1 tablespoon cider vinegar
1 tablespoon chopped dill
1 garlic clove, minced

Salt and pepper, to taste

Directions:

Place the garlic with a pinch of salt in a food blender.
Blend until you have a paste. Gradually add the olive oil until all is emulsified.
Place the chicken in a large bag along with the garlic paste.
Shake and press well until the chicken is nicely coated. Pop in the fridge for 2 hours.
Heat the oven to 420F.
Arrange the lemon slices in the bottom of a baking pan. Top with the chicken and sprinkle with chopped rosemary. Season with salt and pepper.
Roast the chicken for 30 minutes.
Serve while still hot.

Nutritional Info: Per serving

Calories: 417
Total fat: 32.6g

Cholesterol: 36mg
Total Carbs: 11.5g

Protein: 23.3g

AHI POKE BOWLS

Preparation time: 15 minutes

Cooking time: 6 minutes

Servings: 4

Ingredients:

1 lb. sushi grade salmon
¼ cup coconut aminos
2 tablespoons toasted sesame oil
2 tablespoons lime juice
2 teaspoons Sriracha
Salt and pepper, to taste
1 tablespoon black sesame seeds

For the cauli rice:

2 cups cauliflower
4 tablespoons butter
2 tablespoons rice vinegar
Salt, to taste

Additional:

1 avocado, peeled, sliced

Directions:

Slice the salmon into 1-inch pieces and place in a bowl.

Add the remaining ingredients: coconut aminos, sesame seeds oil, lime juice, Sriracha, onions and salt. Stir to combine and cover. Refrigerate for 30 minutes at least.

Prepare the cauliflower rice: process the cauliflower in a food processor until the cauliflower is a rice like structure.

Heat the butter and cook the cauliflower for 5-6 minutes.

Remove from the heat and season with rice vinegar and salt.

Divide the cauliflower rice between bowls and top with salmon. Decorate with avocado slices and sprinkle all with sesame seeds.

Serve after.

Nutritional Info: Per serving

Calories: 345
Total fat: 26.5g

Cholesterol: 81mg
Total Carbs: 3.7g

Protein: 23.5g

UPER FRITTATA

Preparation time: 5 minutes

Cooking time: 35 minutes

Servings: 4

Ingredients:

8 organic eggs
9oz. asparagus spears
2 spring onions, chopped
1 shallot, chopped
1 green bell pepper, seeded, chopped
¼ cup full-fat heavy cream

5.5oz. soft goats cheese
4 tablespoons chopped parsley
2 tablespoons butter or ghee
3.5oz. Pancetta
Salt and pepper, to taste

Directions:

Prepare the veggies as described. Trim the asparagus.

Heat the butter in a large skillet. Add the asparagus, spring onions, shallots, and green bell pepper. Cook the veggies for 5 minutes. Transfer into a baking dish.

In a bowl, whisk the eggs with heavy cream, parsley, salt, and pepper.

Pour the egg mixture over veggies and top with crumbled goats cheese.

Heat the oven to 400F and cook the eggs for 20 minutes. Remove from the oven and top with the Pancetta.

Reduce the heat to 350F and cook the frittata for 15-20 minutes more.

Remove from the oven and place aside to cool. Slice before serving.

Nutritional Info: Per serving

Calories: 363
Total fat: 27.9g

Cholesterol: 290mg
Total Carbs: 6.8g

Protein: 22.4g

SALMON AND CREAMY SPINACH

Preparation time: 10 minutes   Cooking time: 25 minutes   Servings: 4

Ingredients:

4 4.5oz. salmon fillets
1lb. spinach
½ cup heavy whipping cream
4 tablespoons butter
Salt and pepper, to taste

For the sauce:

6 tablespoons butter
4 egg yolks, organic
1 teaspoon mustard
¼ cup lemon juice
2 tablespoons water

Directions:

Prepare the salmon and spinach: heat the oven to 400F. Place the salmon in a baking dish and dot with half the butter. Season to taste. Cook for 20-25 minutes.
Meanwhile, prepare the spinach: heat the remaining butter in a skillet. Add the spinach and season to taste. Cook for 3-5 minutes. Add the heavy whipping cream remove from the heat and place aside.
Prepare the sauce: melt the butter in a water bath and keep aside making sure it is not too hot.
In a glass, heatproof bowl, mix the egg yolks, mustard, lemon juice and water.
Bring 1 cup water to a boil in a saucepot. Keep it on medium heat.
Place the bowl with the egg yolks over the saucepot, making sure the water is not touching the bowl.
Cook the egg yolks over simmering water until thick. Pour in the butter and keep stirring to avoid clumps.
To serve: place the spinach on a plate. Top with baked salmon and drizzle with the egg sauce.

Nutritional Info: Per serving

Calories: 553   Cholesterol: 360mg   Protein: 30.3g
Total fat: 47.1g   Total Carbs: 5.8g

STUFFED AVOCADO

Preparation time: 10 minutes   Cooking time: 25 minutes   Servings: 6

Ingredients:

3 medium avocados, pitted
4 3.5oz. salmon fillets
2 garlic cloves, minced or 1 spring onion, finely chopped
1 cup crème fraiche

¼ cup lemon juice
4 tablespoons melted butter
3 tablespoons chopped dill
Salt and pepper, to taste

Directions:

Heat the oven to 400F and line a baking sheet with parchment paper.
Drizzle with melted butter, half the lemon juice, and season to taste with salt.
Bake the salmon for 20-25 minutes. Place the salmon aside to cool down. Once cooled (5-10 minutes), flake the salmon. Transfer in a bowl and mix with garlic, crème fraiche, remaining lemon juice, and dill.
Scoop the avocado flesh leaving a thin shell. Chop the flesh and combine with the salmon.

Stuff the avocado shells with prepared mixture.
Serve and enjoy.

Nutritional Info: Per serving

Calories: 410

Cholesterol: 58mg

Protein: 15.8g

Total fat: 35.7g

Total Carbs: 10.6g

RIB EYE STEAK WITH PESTO

Preparation time: 10 minutes   Cooking time: 15 minutes   Servings: 4

Ingredients:

0.75lb. rib eye steaks, grass-fed
2 tablespoons butter, softened
Salt and pepper, to taste

For the pesto:

½ cup parsley, chopped
4 garlic cloves, minced
1 tablespoon lemon zest, finely grated
6 tablespoons butter

Directions:

Pat dry the steak with paper towels.
Season the steaks with salt and pepper and top with butter.
Place the steak aside and prepare the pesto: combine all ingredients in a mini blender. Blend for 10 seconds and place aside.
Prepare the steak: heat a grill pan over high heat. Add the steaks and fry 2-3 on each side minutes to close the pores and keep the juices within the meat.
Reduce heat to medium and cook for 7 minutes for medium, or 11 minutes for well done. If you like rare, 4 minutes are enough.
Remove the steaks from the pan and place aside to rest, covered with parchment paper.
Serve with prepared pesto.

Nutritional Info: Per serving

Calories: 381

Cholesterol:138mg

Protein: 30.4g

Total fat: 27.4g

Total Carbs: 1.8g

CHORIZO MEATBALLS WITH CHEESE SAUCE

Preparation time: 10 minutes   Cooking time: 20 minutes   Servings: 4

Ingredients:

½ lb. ground pork
3oz. chorizo sausage, peeled, chopped
1 egg, organic
½ cup almond flour
1 teaspoon ground cumin
2 garlic cloves, minced
1 teaspoon smoked paprika

1 tablespoon butter
Salt and pepper, to taste

For the sauce:

¼ cup heavy cream
2 tablespoons butter
¼ cup cream cheese

½ cup cheddar cheese, grated
Salt and pepper, to taste

Some water, to thin

Directions:

Prepare the meatballs: heat the butter in a skillet. Add the garlic and chorizo and cook for 6-8 minutes. Remove from the heat and place aside.

In a large bowl, combine the ground pork with the egg, almond flour, cumin, smoked paprika, salt, and pepper. Mix to combine and add the chorizo mixture.

Shape the mixture into balls.

Heat the pan where you have cooked the chorizo and ad the meatballs. Cook the meatballs for 2-3 minutes. Turn over and cook for 2 minutes.

Reduce heat and cook for 8-10 minutes.

Meanwhile, prepare the sauce: heat the butter in a saucepot.

Add the cream and once heated add the cream cheese. Stir until melted and bring to a gentle bubble. Remove from the heat and stir in the grated cheddar. Season to taste and mix until creamy. If needed, thin with water. Serve meatballs with prepared sauce.

Nutritional Info: Per serving

Calories: 385
Total fat: 30.5g

Cholesterol:164mg
Total Carbs: 1.9g

Protein: 25.5g

FISH CAKES WITH CREAMY SAUCE

Preparation time: 15 minutes	Cooking time: 10 minutes	Servings: 18 cakes

Ingredients:

8.5oz. cauliflower (processed in a food processor, to resemble the rice)
4 tablespoons coconut oil
1 garlic clove, minced
1.75lb. cod fillets, skinless
1 spring onion, finely chopped
1 teaspoon ground cumin
1 teaspoon lemon zest, finely grated
½ cup grated parmesan
4 tablespoons flax meal

Salt and pepper, to taste

For the sauce:

¾ cup olive oil
1 egg yolk, organic
1 teaspoon mustard
1 tablespoon cider vinegar
1 tablespoon lemon juice
2 garlic cloves, minced
Salt and pepper, to taste

Directions:

Prepare the sauce: in a bowl, whisk the egg yolk and mustard.

While whisking, (by hand or electric whisk), gradually add the oil in a steady thin stream.

Once you have mayonnaise looking mixture, add the remaining ingredients. Whisk until incorporated. Cover and place in a fridge.

Prepare the cauliflower rice: heat 1 tablespoon coconut oil in a skillet. Add the garlic and cook for 30 seconds. Add the cauliflower (processed in a food processor) and cook for 6-8 minute or until crisp-tender. Season to taste and remove from the heat.

Prepare the fish cakes: heat 1 tablespoon coconut oil in a skillet. Add the fish fillets and cook for 3 minutes per side. Flake the fish and place in a bowl. add the remaining ingredients along with the cauliflower rice. Shape 18 patties from the mixture. You can use ¼ cup measure to measure them out and to shape easily. Heat the remaining oil in a skillet. Cook the patties for 4-5 minutes per side, without moving too much. Serve the patties with prepared sauce.

Nutritional Info: Per serving

Calories: 171

Total fat: 13.4g

Cholesterol:38mg

Total Carbs: 1.7g

Protein: 11.0g

TURKEY FRICASSEE

Preparation time: 5 minutes   Cooking time: 15 minutes   Servings: 4

Ingredients:

1lb. turkey meat, from the tights, thinly sliced
3 tablespoons duck fat or lard
2 garlic cloves, minced
1 cup mushrooms, sliced
2 celery stalks, medium, chopped
1 cup chicken broth

2 tablespoons lemon juice
1 cup heavy whipping cream
1 teaspoon smoked paprika
4 egg yolks
2 tablespoons fresh parsley, chopped
Salt and pepper, to taste

Directions:

Heat 2 tablespoons duck fat in a skillet. Add the turkey and cook until browned.
Remove form the skillet and place aside.
Heat 1 tablespoon of the duck fat in the same skillet. Add the garlic. Cook for minute. Add the celery and sliced mushrooms and cook for 6-7 minutes over medium heat.
Add the broth, lemon juice, smoked paprika and bring to a boil. Reduce heat and simmer for 5 minutes.
In a separate bowl, whisk the egg yolks with heavy cream. Slowly drizzle in the turkey mix and season to taste.
Add the parsley and cook for 2 minutes. Place in the turkey and cook for 1 minute.
Serve with cauliflower rice.

Nutritional Info: Per serving

Calories: 458

Total fat: 31.4g

Cholesterol:246mg

Total Carbs: 3.6g

Protein: 28.7g

SPICY SKEWERS

Preparation time: 5 minutes + inactive time   Servings: 6
Cooking time: 15 minutes

Ingredients:

1.5lb. chicken legs, skinless, boneless
1/3 cup Harissa paste

¾ cup olive oil
Salt, to taste

Directions:

Cut the chicken into 1 ½-inch pieces.

Place the chicken in a bowl, with 2 tablespoons olive oil, some salt, and Harissa paste.

Cover and refrigerate for 1 hour. Heat the oven to 440F and prepare baking pan.

Arrange the chicken meat onto skewers and place into a baking pan.

Bake/roast the chicken for 15 minutes. Remove from the oven and let the chicken cool for 5 minutes before serving.

Nutritional Info: Per serving

Calories: 431

Total fat: 33.6g

Cholesterol:101mg

Total Carbs: 0.9g

Protein: 30.8g

FRIED GRAVIERA CHEESE

Preparation time: 10 minutes

Cooking time: 4 minutes

Servings: 2

Ingredients:

5.5oz. Graviera cheese, or Halloumi

3 tablespoons almond meal

3 tablespoons almond meal

¼ cup heavy cream

Oil, to fry

Directions:

Cut the cheese into 1 ½ -inch thick slices.

Pour the cream in a bowl.

In a separate bowl, combine the almond and flax meal.

Dip each cheese slice in a heavy cream then coat with the almond/flax mixture.

Heat ¼-inch oil in the pan. Fry the cheese for 2 minutes per side.

Serve after, with lime wedges.

Nutritional Info: Per serving

Calories: 200

Total fat: 18.0g

Cholesterol:28mg

Total Carbs: 4.2g

Protein: 7.6g

JUICY AND CRISPY PORK

Preparation time: 10 minutes

Cooking time: 40 minutes

Servings: 6

Ingredients:

1lb. pork tenderloin

2 tablespoons bacon fat

2 garlic cloves

4oz. spinach

4oz. cream cheese

1 teaspoon dried thyme

4oz. Gruyere cheese, grated

16 bacon slices, thinly sliced

Salt and pepper, to taste

Directions:

Heat the bacon fat in a skillet. Add the garlic and cook for 30 seconds or until fragrant.

Add the thyme and spinach. Cook until just wilted. Season to taste and stir in the cream cheese. Remove from the heat. Heat the oven to 375F.

Cut the pork tenderloin in half, but not completely. Leave ½-inch of bond between the sides of pork tenderloin. Cover the meat with foil and pound the meat with meat tenderizer, until ½-inch thick.

Create the bacon grid (#) from the bacon strips and place the tenderloin onto the strips. Spread the spinach mix over the pork and sprinkle with grated Gruyere cheese. Roll all together. Secure with toothpicks and transfer the pork onto baking sheet lined with parchment paper, seam side down.

Bake the pork for 40 minutes and for the extra crunchiness broil the pork for 2 minutes.

Let the pork rest for 10 minutes before slicing and serving. Remember to remove toothpicks.

Nutritional Info: Per serving

Calories: 388	Cholesterol: 119mg	Protein: 23.7g
Total fat: 26.8g	Total Carbs: 1.9g	

Herbed Lamb Rack

Preparation time: 10 minutes	Cooking time: 20 minutes	Servings: 8

Ingredients:

2lb. lamb racks or 2 racks, will give 50% meat	1 cup pork rinds, ground
4 tablespoons butter	4 garlic cloves, minced
1 tablespoon mustard	2 sprigs rosemary
	Salt and pepper, to taste

Directions:

Heat the oven to 400F.

Heat 1 tablespoon butter in a large skillet and sear the lamb, fatty side down for 2 minutes. Flip and sear for 30 seconds. Lift with the tongues and sear the bottom an upper side for 30 seconds, per side. Place the lamb aside.

In a food blender, combine the remaining ingredients, except the mustard. Process until crumbly.

Brush the lamb with mustard, fatty part, and cover with prepared crumbly mixture.

Transfer the lamb onto baking tray and bake for 15 minutes for medium-rare or 20 minutes for medium.

Let the lamb rest for 10 minutes before serving.

Nutritional Info: Per serving

Calories: 314	Cholesterol: 128mg	Protein: 22.7g
Total fat: 17.2g	Total Carbs: 1.0g	

Crispy Chicken

Preparation time: 5 minutes	Cooking time: 35 minutes	Servings: 6

Ingredients:

6 3oz. chicken thigs, skin on	½ teaspoon baking soda
1 cup butter	1 ½ teaspoon cream of tartar
1 ½ tablespoons smoked paprika	Salt and pepper, to taste

Directions:

Heat oven to 400F and line a baking sheet with parchment paper.

Pat dry the legs and arrange onto baking sheet or two sheets.

Lift the skin and place the ghee under the skin. Top the chicken with remaining ghee, if any left.

In a bowl, combine the paprika, cream of tartar and baking soda, with salt to taste.

Rub the chicken with prepared mixture and bake for 35 minutes.

Serve after with favorite sauce.

Nutritional Info: Per serving

Calories: 440	Cholesterol: 157mg	Protein: 25.2g
Total fat: 37.2g	Total Carbs: 1.4g	

MEATBALL SKEWERS

Preparation time: 10 minutes	Cooking time: 8 minutes	Servings: 6

Ingredients:

1lb. ground beef

2 garlic cloves, minced

1 egg, organic

1 teaspoon paprika

3 tablespoons chopped fresh basil

7.5oz. chorizo sausage, sliced

Salt and pepper, to taste

Directions:

Combine all ingredients in a bowl, except the chorizo. Cover and refrigerate overnight, but you can use at once.

Form 24 meatballs from the mixture and arrange 3 meatballs onto skewer, with sliced chorizo at the beginning, at the end and in between.

Preheat the grill and grill the meatballs for 8 minutes.

Serve after.

Nutritional Info: Per serving

Calories: 274	Cholesterol: 125mg	Protein: 20.9g
Total fat: 15.6g	Total Carbs: 0.6g	

Keto Snacks

Sweet snacks

Coconut Bombs

Preparation time: 10 minutes   Servings: 6

Ingredients:
4oz. flaked coconut
¼ cup coconut oil, melted

¼ teaspoon vanilla paste
20 drops stevia

Directions:
Preheat oven to 350F and line baking sheet with parchment paper. Spread over coconut flakes and place in the oven. Toast the flakes for 5-8 minutes until golden. Stir once to prevent burning. Transfer in a blender and pulse until smooth. Add the coconut oil, vanilla paste and stevia. Stir to combine. Divide between 12 mini paper cases and place in freezer for 30 minutes. Once firm serve after.

Nutritional Info: Per serving
Calories: 145
Total fat: 15.4g

Cholesterol: 0mg
Total Carbs: 2.9g

Protein: 0.6g

Pecan Bars

Preparation time: 10 minutes   Cooking time: 25 minutes   Servings: 12

Ingredients:
2 cups pecan halves, toasted, crushed
½ cup shredded coconut
½ cup coconut oil, melted
¼ teaspoon stevia, liquid

½ cup almond meal
1 cup almond flour
2 tablespoons almond butter

Directions:
In a bowl combine the almond flour, almond meal and shredded coconut. Add crushed pecans and stir again. Add in remaining ingredients and mix well until you get a crumbly mixture. Line 11x7-inch baking pan with parchment paper and place in the prepared mixture. Press to flatten and bake in preheated oven for 25 minutes at 350F. Remove from the oven and allow to cool. Slice into bars and serve.

Nutritional Info: Per serving
Calories: 230
Total fat: 23.8g

Cholesterol: 0mg
Total Carbs: 4.2g

Protein: 3.4g

PEANUT BUTTER BALLS

Preparation time: 10 minutes + inactive time
Servings: 6

Ingredients:

2 tablespoons heavy cream
4 tablespoons almond butter
2 tablespoon peanut butter, smooth

4 drops stevia
1 ½ teaspoons powdered erythritol

Directions:

In a bowl combine all ingredients. Mix until smooth.
Place in a freezer for 20 minutes. Form into balls and serve.

Nutritional Info: Per serving

Calories: 114
Total fat: 10.5g

Cholesterol: 7mg
Total Carbs: 3.2g

Protein: 3.7g

STRAWBERRY SNACK

Preparation time: 10 minutes + inactive time
Servings: 4

Ingredients:

10 strawberries
¼ cup almond flour
3oz. cream cheese

1 tablespoon powder erythritol
¼ teaspoon vanilla paste

Directions:

In a small bowl combine the cream cheese, vanilla and powder erythritol.
Place the almond flour in a bowl.
Make a small hole in each strawberry and fill with cream cheese. Dip the strawberry tops in almond flour and refrigerate for 20 minutes before serving.

Nutritional Info: Per serving

Calories: 124
Total fat: 11.4g

Cholesterol: 23mg
Total Carbs: 4.4g

Protein: 3.3g

PUMPKIN BOMBS

Preparation time: 10 minutes
Servings: 2

Ingredients:

2 tablespoons coconut oil, melted
½ stick butter, grass-fed, unsalted
½ cup pumpkin puree
1 pinch nutmeg
½ teaspoon allspice

1 pinch cinnamon
5 drops stevia

Directions:

Heat coconut oil in microwave until hot; add butter and whip with fork until blended.
Keep whipping and stir in the pumpkin.
Add the spices and stevia. Place the mixture into fridge until firm. Form balls from the mixture and serve.

Nutritional Info: Per serving

Calories: 343
Total fat: 36.8g

Cholesterol: 61mg
Total Carbs: 5.5g

Protein: 1.0g

CINNAMON CRACKERS

Preparation time: 10 minutes   Cooking time: 25 minutes   Servings: 6

Ingredients:

2 cups almond flour
1 egg
2 tablespoons coconut oil
2 teaspoons vanilla paste

¼ cup erythritol
2 teaspoons cinnamon
1 teaspoon baking soda
1 pinch salt

Directions:

Preheat oven to 300F.In a medium bowl combine the almond flour, erythritol, cinnamon, baking soda and salt. Whisk in the egg, coconut oil and vanilla paste. Mix until you get a cohesive dough.
Place the dough onto large piece of parchment paper; cover with the second one and roll to ¼-inch thick.
Pell off top piece of parchment paper and score the dough into desired shape. Transfer onto baking sheet and bake for 20-25 minutes. Remove from the oven, allow to cool and break up along score marks. Bake for 15 minute more and serve after.

Nutritional Info: Per serving

Calories: 78
Total fat: 7.6g

Cholesterol: 27mg
Total Carbs: 1.7g

Protein: 1.9g

CHEESY RASPBERRIES

Preparation time: 10 minutes
Drying time: 4 hours
Servings: 2

Ingredients:

1 cup cream cheese
¼ cup raspberries + 1 tablespoon
2 tablespoons heavy cream

2 tablespoons powder eyrthritol
2 tablespoons crushed almonds

Directions:

Combine all ingredients in a bowl. Mix until blended.
Divide between bowls and top with remaining raspberries and almonds.
Serve after.

Nutritional Info: Per serving

Calories: 497
Total fat: 46.9g

Cholesterol: 138mg
Total Carbs: 9.1g

Protein: 10.9g

APPLE CHIPS WITH DIP

Preparation time: 10 minutes
Drying time: 2 hours
Servings: 8

Ingredients:

2 apples, medium
2 tablespoons pumpkin pie spice
2 tablespoon powder eyrthritol

1 cup cream cheese
1 tablespoon almond butter
1 tablespoon heavy cream

Directions:

Preheat oven to 400F and line baking sheet with parchment paper.
Using a mandolin, slice the apples very thin. Place the apple slices onto baking sheet.
In a bowl combine the erythritol and pumpkin pie spice; sprinkle all over apple slices.
Bake the apples for 2 hours and serve after.
Combine remaining ingredients to make a dip. Serve apple chips with dip.

Nutritional Info: Per serving

Calories: 154
Total fat: 12.2g

Cholesterol: 138mg
Total Carbs: 8.9g

Protein: 2.9g

VANILLA-MACADAMIA FAT BOMBS

Preparation time: 10 minutes + inactive time   Servings: 8

Ingredients:

1 cup macadamia nuts
1 teaspoon vanilla paste
½ cup coconut oil, melted

10 drops stevia
2 tablespoons powdered erythritol

Directions:

In a food blender pulse the macadamia nuts until smooth.
In a bowl combine the coconut oil with stevia, erythritol and vanilla paste. Stir in processed macadamia nuts and stir to mix well. Spoon the mixture into silicone ice-cube tray and place in freezer for 30 minutes. Pop the sweets from the silicone tray and serve.

Nutritional Info: Per serving

Calories: 238
Total fat: 26.3g
Cholesterol: 0mg

Total Carbs: 2.3g
Protein: 1.3g

COCONUT BITES

Preparation time: 10 minutes   Cooking time: 45 minutes   Servings: 6

Ingredients:

4 egg whites
1 tablespoon powdered erythritol
3 cups desiccated coconut
1pinch salt

To coat:
½ cup melted coconut oil
2 tablespoons cocoa

Directions:

Preheat oven to 350F and line baking sheet with parchment paper.
Whisk the egg whites with 1pinch salt until firm.
Gently stir in the powdered erythritol and coconut.
Form the balls with hands and arrange onto baking sheet.
Bake the coconut balls for 45 minutes or until the balls crackle.
Remove and place aside to cool.
Melt the coconut oil and cocoa powder in a microwave safe bowl. Drizzle the cookies with cocoa. Serve.

Nutritional Info: Per serving

Calories: 310   Cholesterol: 0mg   Protein: 3.8g
Total fat: 31.6g   Total Carbs: 6.2g

WAFFLE STICKS

Preparation time: 5 minutes   Cooking time: 8 minutes   Servings: 2

Ingredients:

6 tablespoons almond flour
2 eggs
½ teaspoon vanilla paste

1 tablespoon erythritol
1 teaspoon cinnamon
¼ teaspoon baking soda

Directions:

In a bowl combine the almond flour, erythritol, ½ teaspoon cinnamon and baking soda.
Whisk in the eggs and vanilla paste.
Preheat waffle iron and pour over prepared batter. Cook the waffle for 3-4 minutes.
Cut waffle into sticks and sprinkle with remaining cinnamon. Serve after.

Nutritional Info: Per serving

Calories: 146   Cholesterol: 164mg   Protein: 8.6g
Total fat: 11.4g   Total Carbs: 4.3g

CRUNCHY ALMOND BUTTER

Preparation time: 5 minutes   Servings: 1

Ingredients:

2 tablespoons almond butter   1 tablespoon pecans, crushed
2 tablespoons crushed almonds

Directions:

Combine all ingredients together. Chill and serve.

Nutritional Info: Per serving

Calories: 265   Cholesterol: 0mg   Protein: 9.3g
Total fat: 23.9g   Total Carbs: 8.6g

AVOCADO-BANANA CACAO COOKIES

Preparation time: 5 minutes   Cooking time: 10 minutes   Servings: 12

Ingredients:

1 cup avocado, diced   1 banana, sliced
½ cup cacao powder, raw   1 egg
4 tablespoons coconut butter   ½ teaspoon baking soda
1 tablespoon erythritol

Directions:

Preheat oven to 350F and line baking sheet with parchment paper.

Combine banana, eyrthritol, coconut butter, and avocado in a bowl.

Mix all until smooth and chunks free. Add the egg, cacao powder and baking soda. Continue mixing until everything is blended.

Drop spoonful of batter onto baking sheet and bake for 8-10 minutes. Place on wire rack to cool and serve after.

Nutritional Info: Per serving

Calories: 78   Cholesterol: 14mg   Protein: 1g
Total fat: 7.3g   Total Carbs: 3.3g

Salty snacks

CUCUMBER MINI SANDWICHES

Preparation time: 5 minutes   Servings: 4

Ingredients:

2 cucumbers, sliced into ¼-inch rounds
2 tablespoons hummus
1 carrot, shredded

4 slices turkey ham
4 slices cheese

Directions:

Spread the hummus over half of the cucumber slices.
Cut the cheese and ham into squares that fit onto cucumber slices.
Top the hummus with carrots, ham and cheese slice. Repeat until you are out of ingredients.
Top with remaining cucumber slices and serve.

Nutritional Info: Per serving

Calories: 186   Cholesterol: 47mg   Protein: 11.2g
Total fat: 12.2g   Total Carbs: 9.2g

ROASTED BRUSSELS SPROUTS CHIPS

Preparation time: 5 minutes   Cooking time: 10 minutes   Servings: 2

Ingredients:

10 Brussels sprouts
¼ teaspoon salt

1 tablespoon olive oil

Directions:

Preheat oven to 350F.
Carefully split the leaves, making sure not to damage. Toss in a bowl with olive oil and place onto rimmed baking sheet. Season with salt and roast for 10 minutes.
Serve while still warm.

Nutritional Info: Per serving

Calories: 161   Cholesterol: 0mg   Protein: 3.2g
Total fat: 14.3g   Total Carbs: 7.6g

JALAPENO POPPERS

Preparation time: 5 minutes   Cooking time: 25 minutes   Servings: 4

Ingredients:

16 jalapenos
16 slices bacon
1 teaspoon salt

1 teaspoon paprika
4oz. cream cheese
¼ cup shredded cheddar cheese

Directions:

Preheat oven to 350F.

Cut bacon in half; cut the jalapenos in half lengthwise.

Mix the cream cheese and cheddar in a bowl.

Fill each jalapeno with cheese mix and wrap around with bacon. Sprinkle with salt and paprika and place into baking dish lined with foil.

Bake the poppers for 25 minutes; serve while still hot.

Nutritional Info: Per serving

Calories: 266   Cholesterol: 66mg   Protein: 13.4g
Total fat: 22.9g   Total Carbs: 1.5g

PIZZA FAT BOMB

Preparation time: 5 minutes   Servings: 6

Ingredients:

2 tablespoons basil, fresh, chopped
4oz. cream cheese
14 slices pepperoni, chopped

8 black olives, pitted, chopped
2 tablespoons sun-dried tomato pesto
Salt and pepper, to taste

Directions:

In a bowl combine the cream cheese, basil and tomato pesto.

Add the chopped pepperoni and olives. Stir to combine.

Form balls from prepared mixture and serve after on a piece of pepperoni slice.

Nutritional Info: Per serving

Calories: 149   Cholesterol:34mg   Protein: 4.5g
Total fat: 14.1g   Total Carbs: 1.0g

CHIA SEED CRACKERS

Preparation time: 5 minutes   Cooking time: 35 minutes   Servings: 8

Ingredients:

3oz. cheddar cheese, shredded
½ cup chia seeds, ground

¼ teaspoon paprika
¼ teaspoon oregano, dried

¼ teaspoon garlic powder
¼ teaspoon salt
¼ teaspoon black pepper

1 ¼ cups water
4 tablespoons olive oil
2 tablespoons almond meal

Directions:

In a bowl combine the chia seeds with almond meal, oregano, paprika, garlic powder, salt and black pepper. Mix well.

Add olive oil and mix until you have consistency of wet sand.

Add water and continue mixing until you get a solid dough. Stir in grated cheese and knead all with clean hands.

Place the dough onto baking sheet and let it rest for few minute. Cover with second piece of parchment paper and roll out to ¼-inch thickness. Remove top layer of the paper and bake in preheated oven for 35 minutes at 375F. Remove from the oven, cut into desired shape and bake for 5-8 minutes more. Place on the wire rack to cool and serve after.

Nutritional Info: Per serving

Calories: 123
Total fat: 12.3g

Cholesterol: 11mg
Total Carbs: 1.1g

Protein: 3.4g

CHEDDAR BISCUITS

Preparation time: 5 minutes   Cooking time: 10 minutes   Servings: 12

Ingredients:

1 ½ cups almond flour
2 eggs
4 cups broccoli florets
¼ cup coconut oil, melted
2 cups cheddar cheese, grated

1 teaspoon salt
1 teaspoon garlic powder
1 teaspoon paprika
½ teaspoon baking soda
½ teaspoon cider vinegar

Directions:

Preheat oven to 375F and line baking sheet with parchment paper.

Pulse broccoli in food processor until finely chopped. Combine with grated cheddar.

In a separate bowl whisk the milk with eggs, cider vinegar and oil. Stir in almond flour, spices and baking soda. Stir until just combined. Add broccoli mix and stir to combine.

Form 12 patties/cookies and arrange onto baking sheet. Bake for 15 minutes, remove from the oven and re-form so they look like real cookies. Bake for 5 minutes more.

Turn oven to broil and broil the cookies for 5 minutes. Remove from the oven and place aside to cool. Serve after.

Nutritional Info: Per serving

Calories: 150
Total fat: 12.8g

Cholesterol: 47mg
Total Carbs: 3.1g

Protein: 7.0g

LOW-CARB CORNDOGS

Preparation time: 5 minutes   Cooking time: 5 minutes   Servings: 4

Ingredients:

4 chicken sausages, pre-cooked
2 tablespoons heavy cream
2 eggs
1 cup almond flour

1 teaspoon baking powder
½ teaspoon salt
½ teaspoon turmeric

Directions:

In a bowl mix together the almond flour and spices.

In a separate bowl whisk the eggs with heavy cream and baking powder. Fold the egg mixture into almond flour mix and stir until well combined.

Heat around 1 cup oil in large pan until reaches 400F. Dip the pre-cooked sausages into almond flour mix and place into heated oil. Fry for 2 minutes per side or until golden.

Serve after.

Nutritional Info: Per serving

Calories: 144
Total fat: 12.2g

Cholesterol: 103mg
Total Carbs: 2.6g

Protein: 7.0g

THYME ZUCCHINI RINGS

Preparation time: 5 minutes   Cooking time: 25 minutes   Servings: 2

Ingredients:

2 zucchinis, peeled, halved
1 ½ cups almond flour
2 tablespoons thyme, fresh, chopped
½ teaspoon salt

½ teaspoon garlic powder
½ teaspoon black pepper
¼ cup butter, softened
2 eggs

Directions:

Preheat oven to 400F.

Remove the core/zucchini seeds with an apple corer. Slice into rings.

Combine the almond flour, thyme, salt, garlic powder and black pepper in a bowl. Whisk the eggs in separate bowl.

Dip each zucchini ring into egg mixture and dredge through flor mix. Arrange the slices onto baking sheet. Dot with softened butter.

Bake in preheated oven for 25 minutes, turning over halfway through. Serve while still hot.

Nutritional Info: Per serving

Calories: 389
Total fat: 35.0g

Cholesterol: 225mg
Total Carbs: 11.5g

Protein: 12.6

AVOCADO FRIES

Preparation time: 5 minutes   Cooking time: 20 minutes   Servings: 4

Ingredients:

2 avocados, sliced into ½-inch wedges
½ cup almond flour
¼ cup sunflower seeds, crushed

1 teaspoon salt
½ teaspoon onion powder
2 eggs, beaten

Directions:

Preheat oven to 450F and line baking sheet with parchment paper.
Whisk the eggs in shallow dish. In separate bowl combine the almond flour, sunflower seeds, and salt and onion powder.
Dip the avocado slices into egg mixture and coat with almond flour mix. Place onto baking sheet and bake for 20 minutes. Serve after.

Nutritional Info: Per serving

Calories: 294
Total fat: 27.8g

Cholesterol: 89mg
Total Carbs: 10.1g

Protein: 8.8g

CAULIFLOWER BITES

Preparation time: 5 minutes   Cooking time: 5 minutes   Servings: 4

Ingredients:

4 cups cauliflower florets
1 cup almond flour
¼ cup Parmesan, grated
2 eggs beaten

1 teaspoon cayenne
1 teaspoon garlic powder
4 tablespoons melted butter

Directions:

In a large bowl combine the almond flour, parmesan, cayenne pepper and garlic powder.
In a separate bowl whisk the eggs.
Dip the cauliflower florets into egg mixture and transfer in a bowl with almond flour mix. Toss to coat well.
Heat 2-inches oil in large skillet. Add cauliflower florets and cook for 2-3 minutes or until evenly golden.
Place on paper towels to drain and serve.

Nutritional Info: Per serving

Calories: 250
Total fat: 20.6g

Cholesterol: 123mg
Total Carbs: 8.3g

Protein: 11.4g

$\mathcal{P}$ARMESAN PUFFS

| Preparation time: 5 minutes | Cooking time: 5 minutes | Servings: 12 |

Ingredients:
½ cup oil, olive
4 egg whites
½ cup Parmesan, grated

1 teaspoon basil, dried
1 pinch salt

Directions:
Whip the egg whites with 1 pinch salt until soft peaks form. Gently fold the parmesan and basil into the egg mixture. Heat olive oil in large skillet and drop the egg white mix by spoon into hot oil.
Cook until browned on all sides, 5 minutes. Serve while still hot.

Nutritional Info: Per serving
| Calories: 102 | Cholesterol: 4mg | Protein: 2.8g |
| Total fat: 10.2g | Total Carbs: 0.3g | |

$\mathcal{B}$EEF JERKY

| Preparation time: 5 minutes | Drying time: 2 hours | Servings: 4 |

Ingredients:
1lb. beef
½ cup coconut amino

½ cup olive oil

Directions:
Slightly freeze the meat so you can slice it nicely to 1/8-inch thick. Place the beef slices in large zip-lock bag and add coconut amino; seal the bag and refrigerate the meat for 2 hours. Preheat oven to 200F and line two baking sheets with aluminum foil and simply place wire rack onto baking sheet.
Place the marinated beef onto wire rack and bake or dehydrate for 2 hours.
Keep in airtight container.

Nutritional Info: Per serving
| Calories: 427 | Cholesterol: 101mg | Protein: 34.4g |
| Total fat: 32.3 | Total Carbs: 1.0g | |

$\mathcal{A}$VOCADO SNACK

| Preparation time: 5 minutes | Servings: 2 |

Ingredients:
1 avocado, cut in quarters

2 tablespoons sunflower seeds, crushed

Directions:
Peel avocado and cut in quarters.
Sprinkle with sunflower seeds and serve immediately.

Nutritional Info: Per serving

Calories: 222

Total fat: 21.1g

Cholesterol: 0mg

Total Carbs: 8.2g

Protein: 3.5g

ROSEMARY ALMONDS

Preparation time: 5 minutes

Cooking time: 2 minutes

Servings: 4

Ingredients:

2 cups almond, blanched

2 tablespoons fresh rosemary, chopped

1 teaspoon salt

4 tablespoons olive oil

1 teaspoon smoked paprika

Directions:

Hat large skillet over medium-high heat.

Coat with olive oil and heat up.

Add the almonds and stir so they do not burn up.

Reduce the heat to low and add salt, paprika and rosemary.

Cook for 2 minutes and place on kitchen towel.

Serve while still warm.

Nutritional Info: Per serving

Calories: 402

Total fat: 38.1g

Cholesterol: 0mg

Total Carbs: 11.5g

Protein: 11.2g

ZUCCHINI FRITTERS

Preparation time: 5 minutes

Cooking time: 5 minutes

Servings: 12

Ingredients:

1 large zucchini, finely grated

1 ½ tablespoons grated parmesan cheese

1 egg, whisked

Dash of chili flakes

Fresh ground salt and pepper – just a pinch

2 tablespoons almond flour

¼ cup coconut oil

Directions:

Place grated zucchinis in clean kitchen towel to remove excess liquid.

Place in a bowl and add remaining ingredients; stir well to combine.

Heat some oil in frying pan and add 1 tablespoon of zucchini mixture per fritter.

Cook fritters in batches, for 2 minutes per side or until golden.

Serve immediately with favorite sauce.

Nutritional Info: Per serving

Calories: 70

Total fat: 6.7g

Cholesterol: 15mg

Total Carbs: 1.5g

Protein: 2.1g

CRISPY BACON FAT BOMBS

Preparation time: 10 minutes   Cooking time: 3 minutes   Servings: 4 bombs

Ingredients:

4 thick bacon slices
4oz. cream cheese
1 green chile, seeded, chopped

1 teaspoon onion powder
Salt and pepper, to taste

Directions:

Heat the non-stick skillet over medium-high heat. Cook the bacon in the skillet until crispy. Transfer onto paper towel and crumble. Keep the bacon fat. In a bowl, combine the cream cheese, green chile, onion powder, salt, and pepper. Stir until just combined. Add the bacon fat and mix until evenly mixed.

Shape the mixture into four fat bombs. Place the crumbled bacon onto plate and roll the fat bombs into the bacon. Serve after or chill slightly before serving.

Nutritional Info: Per serving

Calories: 135   Cholesterol: 38mg   Protein: 4.5g
Total fat: 12.5g   Total Carbs: 1.3g

MEXICAN FRIED CHEESE

Preparation time: 10 minutes   Cooking time: 10 minutes   Servings: 4

Ingredients:

6oz. Mexican soft cheese, like Queso
Blanco
2 tablespoons olive oil

¼ teaspoon red pepper flakes
3oz. pitted green or black olives, to serve
with

Directions:

Cut the cheese in cubes and place on a plate lined with parchment paper.

Pop the cubes in a freezer for 10 minutes.

Heat the olive oil in a medium sized skillet.

Place the cheese cubes into skillet and sprinkle with red pepper flakes. Reduce the heat and try to brown the cheese on all sides. We suggest that you cut the cheese in bigger cubes.

Once the cheese is browned, bring it all together and press with a spatula to bod it all together.

Cook the cheese for 10 seconds then flip in half. Press the cheese again with the spatula and continue cooking for 10 seconds.

Flip the cheese again and continue pressing and flipping until cheese has a nice crust. With a help of other spatula, shape the cheese mixture into block, with sealed edges.

Remove the cheese from the skillet and place aside for 5-10 minutes.

Cut the cheese into cubes and serve with olives.

Nutritional Info: Per serving

Calories: 237   Cholesterol: 38mg   Protein: 9.3g
Total fat: 23.0g   Total Carbs: 2.9g

Mozzarella Bacon Bites

Preparation time: 15 minutes   Cooking time: 10 minutes   Servings: 20 bites

Ingredients:

10oz. mozzarella cheese
4 tablespoons almond meal
¼ cup melted butter, unsalted
1 large egg

3 tablespoons ground flax seeds
10 slices bacon
Salt and pepper, to taste
1 cup lard, to fry

Directions:

Shred the mozzarella cheese and place half the cheese in a microwave safe bowl.
Microwave the cheese until melted and gooey. Add the melted butter and the egg and stir until combined.
Add the almond meal, flax seeds, and season to taste. At this point you can add some other spices.
Mix until you have a dough and transfer onto silicone mat or piece of parchment paper. Shape the dough into rectangle, ¼-inch thick. Spread the remaining mozzarella over the dough, leaving 1-inch border free. Fold the dough over the cheese and pinch down the edges. Reshape the entire dough so it has a nice square form. Cut the dough into 20 mini squares. Cut each bacon slice in half. Wrap the prepared mozzarella cubes with the bacon and secure with a toothpick. Heat the lard in a saucepot. Add prepared wrapped snacks and fry until the bacon is crispy. Place onto paper towels to drip before serving.

Nutritional Info: Per serving/ball

Calories: 186   Cholesterol: 36mg   Protein: 5.9g
Total fat: 17.6g   Total Carbs: 1.1g

Egg Bacon Snack

Preparation Time: 10 minutes
Cooking time: 10 minutes   Servings: 6

Ingredients:

6 medium eggs
¼ cup mayonnaise
1 tablespoon bacon fat
3 slices bacon

2 teaspoons mustard
Salt and pepper, to taste
Chopped chives, to sprinkle

Directions:

Cook the eggs in simmering water until hardboiled. It takes around 7-8 minutes. Let the eggs sit in hot water for 5 minutes more. Place the cooked eggs in a cold water and let them rest for 30 minutes. Peel the eggs after. Chop the bacon and cook in a non-stick skillet until crispy. Cut the eggs in half by length and scoop the yolks. In a bowl, mash the yolks with bacon fat, mayonnaise and mustard. Season to taste. Fill the empty egg white shells with bacon. Top with egg yolk mix and sprinkle with chives before serving. Enjoy.

Nutritional Info: Per serving

Calories: 143   Cholesterol: 172mg   Protein: 7.1g
Total fat: 11.4g   Total Carbs: 3.1g

PISTACHIO CHEESE BALLS

Preparation time: 10 minutes   Servings: 6 balls

Ingredients:

5oz. goats cheese, semisoft
½ cup pistachios, finely chopped

½ tablespoon sun-dried tomatoes, chopped
Salt and pepper, to taste

Directions:

In a bowl, combine the goats cheese, sun-dried tomatoes, salt and pepper. Place the pistachios in a shallow plate. Shape the cheese mixture into six balls and roll through the pistachios.
Once the balls are fully covered serve and enjoy.

Nutritional Info: Per serving

Calories: 134   Cholesterol: 25mg   Protein: 8.2g
Total fat: 10.8g   Total Carbs: 1.9g

CHEESY PEPPERONI BALLS

Preparation time: 10 minutes   Servings: 6 balls

Ingredients:

5oz. cream cheese
2 tablespoons pureed sun-dried tomatoes
8 black olives, pitted and chopped

1.5oz. pepperoni slices, chopped + 6 slices (un-chopped)
1 tablespoon fresh basil, chopped
Salt and pepper, to taste

Directions:

In a bowl, combine all the ingredients by order. Season to taste and stir to blend.
Shape the mixture into six balls. Serve the balls onto pepperoni slices.

Nutritional Info: Per serving

Calories: 137   Cholesterol: 36mg   Protein: 4.0g
Total fat: 13.0g   Total Carbs: 1.2g

ROASTED BROCCOLI WITH CREAMY DIP

Preparation time: 5 minutes   Cooking time: 25 minutes   Servings: 4

Ingredients:

4 cups broccoli florets
1 tablespoon olive oil
Salt and pepper, to taste

½ cup mozzarella, shredded
3 tablespoon mayonnaise
¼ cup tomato sauce
½ cup parmesan cheese

For the dip:

5oz. cream cheese
¼ cup sour cream

Directions:

Heat the oven to 375F. Arrange the broccoli florets onto baking sheet. Drizzle with olive oil and season to taste. Place the broccoli in the oven, leaving some space.

In a bowl, combine the cream cheese, sour cream, mozzarella, and mayonnaise. Divide the mixture between four ramekins. Top each with tomato paste and sprinkle with parmesan.

Pop in the oven with the broccoli. Bake the cheese dip for 20 minutes and the broccoli for 25 minutes. Serve at room temperature.

Nutritional Info: Per serving

Calories: 320
Total fat: 26.7g

Cholesterol: 61mg
Total Carbs: 10.7g

Protein: 11.8g

SALTED CARAMEL BACON BITES

Preparation time: 15 minutes   Cooking time: 30 minutes   Servings: 24 bites

Ingredients:

5 eggs, separated
½ cup powdered Erythritol
½ teaspoon vanilla paste
1 teaspoon maple extract
2 tablespoons coconut oil
¼ teaspoon liquid stevia
For the sauce:
6 tablespoons butter
6 tablespoons heavy cream

2 tablespoons flax seeds flour
1 cup almond flour
2 tablespoons butter, softened
1 teaspoon baking powder
½ teaspoon cream of tartar

3 tablespoons chopped sugar free caramels

Directions:

Heat oven to 325F and line a 8-inch baking sheet with a parchment paper.

Separate the eggs (yolks and whites) in two mixing bowls. In the owl where the yolks are, add the powdered eyrthritol, vanilla paste, maple extract, coconut oil, and stevia.

Beat with an electric whisk until pale. Stir in the flax seeds flour, almond flour, butter, and baking soda. When you have a smooth batter, stir in the ¾ of the bacon.

Beat the egg whites with cream of tartar until soft peaks form. Stir 1/3 of the egg whites into bacon batter and stir until blended. Repeat until you use all the egg whites. Transfer the batter into baking sheet. Bake the sponge for 25 minutes.

Meanwhile, prepare the sauce; melt the butter in a saucepan. Cook in until browned and add the heavy cream and caramels.

Mix everything and cook until slightly reduced.

Slice the baked sponge into 24 pieces. Dip each piece in a prepared sauce and arrange onto plate, lined with parchment paper. Sprinkle with remaining bacon and serve.

Nutritional Info: Per serving

Calories: 79
Total fat: 8.0g

Cholesterol: 49mg
Total Carbs: 0.7g

Protein: 1.6g

Avocado Fat Bombs

Preparation time: 30 minutes   Servings: 6

Ingredients:

2oz. butter, softened
3.5oz. avocado
1 tablespoon lime juice
2 garlic cloves, minced
2 tablespoons cilantro, chopped

1 jalapeno, seeded, chopped
4.2oz. bacon, cooked, crumbled (reserve bacon grease)
Salt and pepper, to taste

Directions:

Peel, pit, and slice the avocado. Place the avocado in a bowl with butter, lime juice, garlic, cilantro, jalapeno, salt, and pepper. Mash the ingredients with a fork. Pour in the reserved bacon grease and stir to combine. Cover and refrigerate for 20 minutes. Place the crumbled bacon in a plate. Form six balls from the chilled avocado mix (use ice cream scoop) and roll in the bacon. Chill additional for 5-10 minutes and serve.

Nutritional Info: Per serving

Calories: 210   Cholesterol: 42mg   Protein: 7.8g
Total fat: 19.2g   Total Carbs: 2.0g

Cheesy Crisps with dip

Preparation time: 5 minutes   Cooking time: 10 minutes   Servings: 4

Ingredients:

7.5oz. grated Parmesan cheese
1 teaspoon curry powder
4 tablespoons almond flour

For the dip:

½ cup mayo
1 garlic clove, minced
½ tablespoon capers
1 teaspoon Sriracha

Salt and pepper, to taste

Directions:

Heat oven to 350F. Line a baking sheet with parchment paper and for better orientation (if needed) draw small circles on the paper. In a bowl, combine the Parmesan cheese, oregano, garlic powder, and almond flour. Scoop a teaspoon of cheese mixture and place onto a parchment paper. This is the part where the circles may help. Keep in mind to leave 1-inch space between.
Bake the crisps for 10 minutes.
In the meantime prepare the dip; combine all the dip ingredients in a food blender. Blend on high. Transfer into a bowl and chill slightly before serving.
Place aside to cool and once cooled peel from the paper. Serve after with the dip.

Nutritional Info: Per serving

Calories: 330   Cholesterol: 46mg   Protein:19.0g
Total fat: 24.8g   Total Carbs: 10.3g

Bacon Wrapped Brussels Sprouts

Preparation time: 5 minutes   Cooking time: 15 minutes   Servings: 4

Ingredients:

0.5 lb. Brussels sprouts
7 oz. thick cut bacon
Fresh ground pepper
Fresh ground salt

1 teaspoon rosemary, chopped
2 tablespoon olive oil
1 teaspoon smoked paprika

Directions:

Heat oven to 420F and line baking tray with parchment paper.
Season Brussels sprouts with salt and pepper. Add rosemary, smoked paprika, and olive oil.
Toss to combine. Cut the bacon slices in halves and wrap around sprouts.
Secure with toothpick.
Arrange onto baking sheet and bake for 15 minutes. Serve after.

Nutritional Info: Per serving

Calories: 355
Total fat: 28.0g

Cholesterol: 55mg
Total Carbs: 6.4g

Protein: 20.4g

Avocado-Tuna Bites

Preparation time: 5 minutes   Cooking time: 5 minutes   Servings: 4

Ingredients:

10oz. can tuna, drained
1/3 cup almond flour
1 avocado, peeled, diced
¼ cup mayonnaise

¼ cup parmesan, grated
½ teaspoon salt
¼ teaspoon garlic powder

Directions:

In a bowl combine the tuna with mayonnaise, parmesan and spices.
Add the diced avocado and stir to combine.
Spread the almond flour in shallow dish. Form 12 balls from the mixture and roll in almond flour.
Heat 2-inch oil in large skillet; add prepared balls and cook until browned on all sides. Place on paper towel to drain, before serving.

Nutritional Info: Per serving

Calories: 380
Total fat: 27.2g

Cholesterol: 37mg
Total Carbs: 10.0g

Protein: 26.2g

Ketogenic Burgers - Lunch and Dinner Bonus Recipes

BEEF AND BACON BURGER

Preparation time: 5 minutes   Cooking time: 10 minutes   Servings: 6

Ingredients:

1lb. ground beef
6 slices bacon, cooked
1 ½ teaspoons fish sauce
8oz. burratta cheese, sliced

Salt and pepper, to taste
Fresh baby spinach leaves
6 low-carb burger buns

Directions:

In a large bowl, combine the meat, fish sauce, salt and pepper. Mix well with clean hands and form 4 balls. Place a piece of buratta on the center of two of the patties. Take the other two patties and place them over the cheese. Pinch the edges to seal and refrigerate for 15 minutes. Preheat the grill and season burgers additional with salt and pepper. Grill the burgers for 5 minutes on both sides. Remove the burgers from direct heat and cook over indirect heat for 5 minutes more per side. Let the burgers rest for 3 minutes.
Serve burgers with toasted buns, remaining cheese, and spinach leaves.

Nutritional Info: Per serving

Calories: 328
Total fat: 19.9g

Cholesterol: 114mg
Total Carbs: 0.7g

Protein: 24.8g

CHICKEN BURGERS

Preparation time: 5 minutes   Cooking time: 10 minutes   Servings: 6

Ingredients:

1 ½ lb. ground chicken
4 tablespoon chopped cilantro
2 garlic cloves, minced
2 teaspoons chopped jalapeno
1 teaspoon smoked paprika

1 teaspoon smoked cumin
1/3 cup shredded cheddar cheese
Salt and pepper, to taste
2 avocados, sliced
6 low-carb burger buns, toasted

Directions:

Preheat the grill.

In a bowl, combine all the ingredients, from chicken to cheddar cheese. Season with salt and pepper to taste. Mix the ingredients with clean hands until thoroughly blended.

Form the mixture into four ½-inch thick patties. Grill the burgers for 5-6 minutes per side.

Serve with avocado slices and toasted buns.

Nutritional Info: Per serving

Calories: 380   Cholesterol: 108mg   Protein: 25.8g
Total fat: 23.6g   Total Carbs: 6.4g

SALMON BURGERS WITH AIOLI

Preparation time: 5 minutes   Cooking time: 15 minutes   Servings: 6

Ingredients:

1 ¾ lb. salmon, cut into pieces
3 tablespoons mayonnaise
1 egg
2 tablespoons lemon juice
1 garlic clove, minced
2 tablespoons cilantro, chopped
¼ teaspoon dried dill weed
1/3 cup blanched almond flour
Salt and pepper, to taste
6 low-carb burger buns, toasted

For the aioli:

2 egg yolks
2 teaspoons lemon juice
½ cup olive oil
2 garlic cloves, minced
½ teaspoon mustard
½ teaspoon dill weed
Salt, to taste

Directions:

In a food blender combine the salmon with the mayonnaise, egg, lemon juice and garlic.

Pulse until blended thoroughly. Transfer into a bowl.

Add the remaining ingredients and stir with a wooden spoon to combine. Form 6 patties from the mixture.

Preheat non-stick skillet over medium-high heat. Coat the skillet with some coconut oil.

Fry the patties for 3-4 minutes per side. Place aside and keep warm.

Prepare the aioli: combine the garlic and some salt. Mix until you have a paste.

Combine the garlic paste with remaining ingredients and using immersion blender, blend until emulsified.

Serve warm patties with toasted buns. Drizzle the patties with aioli and enjoy.

Nutritional Info: Per serving

Calories: 382   Cholesterol: 157mg   Protein: 26.8
Total fat: 29.8g   Total Carbs: 2.9g

GARLIC BEEF BURGERS

Preparation time: 5 minutes   Cooking time: 10 minutes   Servings: 6

Ingredients:

1 ½ lb. ground beef
1 tablespoon melted butter
8 bacon strips
1 head garlic, unpeeled
1 tablespoon minced parsley

½ teaspoon fresh sage, chopped
6 slices gouda cheese
1 tablespoon Worcestershire sauce
Salt and pepper, to taste
6 low-carb buns, toasted

Directions:

Preheat oven to 350F and line a rimmed baking sheet with parchment paper.
Arrange the bacon on a baking sheet and wrap the garlic in aluminum foil.
Bake the bacon for 30 minutes and remove from the oven. Continue baking garlic for 15 minutes longer.
Once the garlic is cold enough to handle, squeeze it from the peel in a bowl.
Add in the beef, butter, parsley, sage, and Worcestershire sauce. Season to taste.
Mix with clean hands until blended thoroughly. Form 4 patties from the beef mixture.
Preheat the grill. Grill the patties for 5 minutes. Flip carefully and cook for 4 minutes more.
In the last minutes of cooking, top the patties with cheese slices and let them melt.
Serve patties with toasted buns.

Nutritional Info: Per serving

Calories: 330   Cholesterol: 138mg   Protein: 31.4g
Total fat: 16.7g   Total Carbs: 1.2g

LAMB BURGERS

Preparation time: 5 minutes   Cooking time: 10 minutes   Servings: 4

Ingredients:

½ lb. ground lamb
¼ lb. ground beef
4oz. crumbled goats cheese
1 tablespoon balsamic vinegar
1 ½ tablespoons chopped basil
4 low-carb buns

For the sauce:

4 tablespoons Greek yogurt
1 cucumber, grated
2 garlic cloves, minced
1 teaspoon olive oil
1 teaspoon dill weed, chopped
Salt and pepper, to taste

Directions:

In a large bowl, combine the lamb, beef, balsamic vinegar, and basil in a bowl.
Mix with clean hands. Add the cheese and basil. Season with hands and stir few times.
Preheat the grill. Grill the patties for 4 minutes per side. Keep warm, while you prepare the sauce.
In a bowl, combine all the sauce ingredients. Stir well, until blended thoroughly.
Serve patties with burger buns and prepared sauce.

Nutritional Info: Per serving

Calories: 312

Cholesterol: 106mg

Protein: 33.8g

Total fat: 17.3g

Total Carbs: 4.1g

TURKEY ZUCCHINI BURGERS

Preparation time: 5 minutes

Cooking time: 10 minutes

Servings: 4

Ingredients:

1lb. ground turkey
1 grated zucchini, liquid squeezed
1 egg
2 tablespoons chopped flat-leaf parsley
2 tablespoons chopped cilantro
2 garlic cloves, minced
½ teaspoon ground cumin

Salt and pepper, to taste
4 low-carb burger buns, toasted

For the lime sauce:

7oz. Greek yogurt
2 tablespoon olive oil
1 lime, juiced
Salt and pepper, to taste

Directions:

Squeeze the grated zucchini to remove excess liquid.

Combine the zucchini with ground turkey, egg, parsley, cilantro, garlic, and cumin. Season to taste and stir until blended thoroughly. Cover and refrigerate for 15 minutes.

Meanwhile, prepare the sauce: combine all the sauce ingredients in a bowl. Chill until ready to use. Preheat the grill.

Form four patties form the prepared mixture. Grill for 5 minutes per side.

Serve patties, drizzled with sauce and with toasted buns.

Nutritional Info: Per serving

Calories: 346

Cholesterol: 159g

Protein: 28.2g

Total fat: 21.7g

Total Carbs: 4.5g

PORK BURGERS

Preparation time: 5 minutes

Cooking time: 10 minutes

Servings: 6

Ingredients:

1lb. ground pork shoulder
2 garlic cloves, minced
1 ½ teaspoons chili powder
1 teaspoon cayenne pepper
1 teaspoon red wine vinegar
½ teaspoon dried basil
¼ teaspoon ground cumin
Salt and pepper, to taste
6 low-carb burger buns, toasted
½ cup shredded manchego cheese

For the sauce:

4 tablespoons mayonnaise
1 ½ teaspoons smoked paprika
¼ teaspoon chili powder
1 teaspoon yellow mustard
1 lime, juiced

Directions:

Prepare the sauce: combine all the ingredients in a small bowl.

Cover and chill until ready to use.

Prepare the patties: in a large bowl, combine all the ingredients. Season to taste.

Stir the ingredients with clean hands until blended. Preheat grill and form 4 patties. Grill the patties for 4 minutes. Flip the patties and sprinkle with cheese. Grill for 3 minutes.

Serve patties on toasted bins and drizzle with prepared sauce before serving.

Nutritional Info: Per serving

Calories: 162

Total fat: 7.2g

Cholesterol: 58mg

Total Carbs: 3.7g

Protein: 10.2g

CHILE CHICKEN BURGERS

Preparation time: 5 minutes   Cooking time: 10 minutes   Servings: 6

Ingredients:

6 chicken legs, skinless, boneless

½ cup fresh cilantro, chopped

1 chile pepper, seeded and minced

2 teaspoons garlic powder

1 celery stalk, chopped

3 medium slices bacon, chopped

4 tablespoons olive oil

Salt and pepper, to taste

6 low-carb burger buns

Directions:

Chop the chicken into a bite size pieces.

Place the chicken in a food blender, along with the remaining ingredients.

Process until blended, but not mushy.

Form four patties from the mixture.

Preheat the grill. Grill the patties for 5 minutes per side.

Serve after, with low-carb buns.

Nutritional Info: Per serving

Calories: 180

Total fat: 13.8g

Cholesterol: 41mg

Total Carbs: 0.9g

Protein: 13.4g

BUFFALO BURGERS

Preparation time: 5 minutes   Cooking time: 10 minutes   Servings: 4

Ingredients:

1lb. ground beef

Salt and pepper, to taste

1 teaspoon chili powder

4 low-carb burger buns

For the topping:

4 tablespoons olive oil

3 jalapeno peppers, sliced

2 garlic cloves, minced

1/3 cup hot sauce

Directions:

Prepare the topping: heat olive oil in a skillet.

Add garlic and cook until fragrant. Toss in the sliced jalapeno and cook for 1 minute.

Add hot sauce and simmer for 5 minutes. Reduce from the heat and place aside.

Prepare the burgers: combine the beef with chili powder, salt, and pepper.

Shape the beef into four patties. Grill the patties for 5 minutes per side or until desired doneness is reached.

Serve patties on a burger buns and top with prepared topping. Enjoy.

Nutritional Info: Per serving

Calories: 342	Cholesterol: 101mg	Protein: 24.8g
Total fat: 21.4g	Total Carbs: 2.0g	

ZUCCHINI LAMB PATTIES

Preparation time: 5 minutes   Cooking time: 10 minutes   Servings: 4

Ingredients:

1lb. ground lamb
2 small zucchinis, grated
1 teaspoon garlic powder
½ teaspoon salt
¼ teaspoon cayenne pepper

1 tablespoon onion flakes
1 teaspoon celery flakes
2 tablespoons dried parsley
½ teaspoon dried thyme
4 low-carb burger buns

Directions:

Squeeze the zucchinis to remove excess liquid.

In a bowl, combine the lamb, zucchinis, garlic, salt, cayenne pepper, onion flakes, celery flakes, parsley, and thyme.

With a clean hands, combine the ingredients until blended thoroughly.

Shape the mixture into 12 small patties.

Preheat the grill and cook patties for 2 minutes per side. Serve while still hot, with sliced burger buns.

Nutritional Info: Per serving

Calories: 228	Cholesterol: 102mg	Protein: 12.9g
Total fat: 9.5g	Total Carbs: 3.8g	

CHEESE TURKEY BURGERS WITH DILL CUCUMBER

Preparation time: 5 minutes   Cooking time: 15 minutes   Servings: 6

Ingredients:

1lb. ground turkey
1 zucchini, grated
4oz. Havarti Cheese
Salt and pepper, to taste
6 low-carb Burger buns, toasted

For the topping:

1 Lebanese cucumber, thinly sliced
3 garlic cloves, minced
1 cup white wine vinegar
1 teaspoon dried dill weed

Directions:

Prepare the topping: in a small bowl, combine the cucumbers, garlic, and the dill weed. Pour over vinegar and cover. Refrigerate until ready to use.

Prepare the burgers: squeeze the grated zucchinis to remove excess liquid.

Add the ground turkey and season to taste. Mix well with clean hands and form four patties from the mixture. Preheat the grill and cook the patties for 8-9minutes per side.

Top each burger with sliced cheese and cook for 1 minute or until the cheese is all gooey and melted.

Serve the patties with toasted burger buns and sliced cucumbers.

Nutritional Info: Per serving

Calories: 246

Cholesterol: 97mg

Protein: 23.6g

Total fat: 14.5g

Total Carbs: 4.5g

CHIPOTLE BURGERS

Preparation time: 5 minutes

Cooking time: 15 minutes

Servings: 4

Ingredients:

1lb. ground beef
2 chipotle peppers, minced
¾ tablespoon adobo sauce
1 teaspoon salt
1 teaspoon black pepper

1 teaspoon ground coriander seeds
4 slices Jack Monterey Cheese
2 avocados, peeled, pitted and sliced
2 Poblano chile peppers, roasted
4 low-carb burger buns, toasted

Directions:

In a bowl, combine the beef with minced chipotle peppers, adobo sauce, salt, black pepper, and coriander seeds. Start mixing with clean hands until blended.

Shape mixture into four patties. Preheat the grill.

Cook the patties for 6-8 minutes per side. Top each burger with a slice of cheese and cook for 1 minute more. Meanwhile, toast the buns and top with sliced avocado. Serve the patties on avocado and top with sliced roasted Poblano chile peppers. Enjoy.

Nutritional Info: Per serving

Calories: 430

Cholesterol: 101mg

Protein: 26.8g

Total fat: 27.7g

Total Carbs: 12.1g

GREEN CHILE CHEESEBURGERS

Preparation time: 5 minutes

Cooking time: 15 minutes

Servings: 4

Ingredients:

1lb. ground beef
¼ teaspoon garlic powder
¼ teaspoon hot sauce
Salt and pepper, to taste

Additionally:

4 slices Jack Pepper Cheese
4oz. sliced green chiles
4 low-carb burger buns

Directions:

Prepare the patties: in a bowl, combine all the ingredients. Mix well with clean hands. Shape the mixture into four patties. Preheat the grill and cook the patties for 6-8 minutes per side. Top the patties with sliced Jack Pepper cheese. Cook for 1 minute or until the cheese is melted. Meanwhile, toast the buns and top with prepared patties. Add the green chiles and serve immediately. Enjoy.

Nutritional Info: Per serving

Calories: 334

Cholesterol: 131mg

Protein: 31.4g

Total fat: 16.4g

Total Carbs: 2.4g

SPICY TURKEY BURGERS

Preparation time: 5 minutes

Cooking time: 10 minutes

Servings: 4

Ingredients:

1lb. ground turkey
¼ cup chopped fresh cilantro
1 teaspoon dry harissa seasoning
2 teaspoons olive oil
¼ teaspoon ground coriander seeds
Salt and pepper, to taste

4 slices Cheddar cheese
4 low-carb burger buns

For the Harissa sauce:

4 tablespoons mayonnaise
1 teaspoon harissa paste
¼ teaspoon garlic powder

Directions:

Prepare the Harissa sauce: combine all the ingredients. Mix well and refrigerate until ready to use. Prepare the burgers: in a bowl, combine all ground turkey, cilantro, dry harissa, olive oil, and coriander seeds. Season to taste and give it all a good stir until blended. Shape the prepared mixture into a four patties. Preheat the grill and cook the patties for 4-6 minutes per side. Top the patties with sliced cheddar cheese and cook until the cheese is melted. It usually takes 1 or 2 minutes. Meanwhile, toast the buns. Spread the harissa sauce over buns and top with grilled patties. Serve immediately and enjoy.

Nutritional Info: Per serving

Calories: 412

Cholesterol: 149

Protein: 28.2g

Total fat: 29.0g

Total Carbs: 4.1g

PROVOLONE CHEESEBURGERS

Preparation time: 5 minutes

Cooking time: 15 minutes

Servings: 4

Ingredients:

For the burgers:

1lb. ground beef
2 teaspoons olive oil
1 teaspoon dried thyme
1 tablespoon Worcestershire sauce
Salt and pepper, to taste

Additionally:

½ cup coarse ground white pepper
4 slices Provolone cheese
4 low-carb burger buns

Directions:

Preheat the grill.

Combine all the burger ingredients in a bowl.

Shape prepared burger mixture into four patties. Spoon white pepper on each patty evenly, both sides.

Grill the patties for 6-8 minutes pre side. Top the patties with Provolone cheese and cook for 2 minutes.

Meanwhile, toast the buns. Serve the grilled patties with buns while still hot.

Nutritional Info: Per serving

Calories: 333

Total fat: 16.9g

Cholesterol: 121mg

Total Carbs: 1.5g

Protein: 31.6g

Burgers with Avocado Salsa

Preparation time: 5 minutes   Cooking time: 10 minutes   Servings: 4

Ingredients:

1lb. fresh salmon fillets

½ cup almond flour

1 egg

2 green onions, chopped

1 tablespoon lime juice

½ jalapeno pepper, seeded, minced

Salt and pepper, to taste

4 low-carb burger buns

For the salsa:

1 avocado, chopped

1 tablespoon lime juice

½ jalapeno pepper, seeded and chopped

Salt and pepper, to taste

Directions:

Prepare the salsa: combine all the salsa ingredients in a bowl. Place aside.

Prepare the burgers: Skin the salmon fillets and chop finely.

Place the chopped salmon in a food blender. Add the remaining ingredients and buzz few times.

Transfer into a bowl and stir once or twice just to blend the ingredients.

Shape the mixture into 4 patties. Preheat the grill.

Cook the patties for 4 minutes per side. Serve patties with buns and top with prepared salsa.

Enjoy.

Nutritional Info: Per serving

Calories: 312

Total fat: 21.4g

Cholesterol: 91mg

Total Carbs: 6.7g

Protein: 25.0g

Tuna Burgers with Anchovy Aioli

Preparation time: 5 minutes   Cooking time: 15 minutes   Servings: 4

Ingredients:

1lb. tuna, diced

¼ cup olives, chopped

1 scallion, sliced thinly

1 tablespoon olive oil

Salt and pepper, to taste

4 burger buns, low carb

For the Anchovy aioli:
1 egg yolk

¼ cup extra virgin olive oil
2 tablespoons lemon juice
1 teaspoon anchovy paste

Directions:

In a large bowl, combine the tuna, olives, and scallion. Cover and refrigerate for 10 minutes.

Whet the 10 minutes are up, transfer the tuna mix into a food blender.

Pulse until the tuna is finely chopped. Form four patties from the mixture and brush each with olive oil.

Preheat the grill to medium-high.

Cook the patties for 4-5 minutes per side.

Meanwhile, prepare the aioli: in a jug combine the egg yolk, olive oil, salt, pepper, and lemon juice. Using an immersion blender, blend the ingredients until emulsified. Stir in the anchovy paste.

Brush the tuna patties with prepared aioli. Serve patties with toasted buns.

Nutritional Info: Per serving

Calories: 378   Cholesterol: 92mg   Protein: 21.1g
Total fat: 29.1g   Total Carbs: 1.1g

Bun-less Burger

Preparation time: 5 minutes   Cooking time: 10 minutes   Servings: 6

Ingredients:

1 ½ lb. ground chicken meat
2 teaspoons olive oil
2 garlic cloves, minced
¼ cup chopped Italian parsley

Salt and pepper, to taste
8 Portobello mushrooms
6 slices Provolone cheese

Directions:

Heat 1 teaspoon olive oil in a small pan.

Add the garlic, and cook until fragrant. Transfer into a bowl.

Add the chicken into a bowl and remaining oil. Season to taste and stir in the parsley.

Mix with clean hands until blended. Preheat the grill.

Shape the mixture into four patties.

Brush the patties and mushroom caps with some olive oil and grill.

For the patties 5 minutes per side and for the mushrooms 4 minutes per side.

Top the patties with cheese and cook for 1 minute or until melted.

Arrange the patties onto half of the mushrooms cheese side up. Sandwich with remaining mushrooms and serve.

Nutritional Info: Per serving

Calories: 290   Cholesterol: 107mg   Protein: 15.9g
Total fat: 12.6g   Total Carbs: 1.9g

PORK AND APPLE BURGERS

Preparation time: 5 minutes   Cooking time: 15 minutes   Servings: 4

Ingredients:

1lb. ground pork
1 egg
2 tablespoons chopped coriander
1 teaspoon Worcestershire sauce
2 garlic cloves, chopped
4 slices mozzarella cheese

1 apple, peeled, cored and cut into 4 rounds
Salt and pepper, to taste
4 tablespoons olive oil
4 low-carb burger buns

Directions:

In a bowl, combine the pork with egg, coriander, Worcestershire sauce, and garlic. Season to taste.
Shape the mixture into eight patties. Preheat the grill.
Place the apple and cheese slices on half the patties. Top with remaining patties and pinch edges to seal.
Brush the patties with olive oil and the grill as well. Grill the patties for 8 minutes pre side.
Serve with toasted buns and enjoy.

Nutritional Info: Per serving

Calories: 411   Cholesterol: 139mg   Protein: 19.9g
Total fat: 24.2g   Total Carbs: 9.6g

VEAL PARMESAN BURGERS

Preparation time: 5 minutes   Cooking time: 10 minutes   Servings: 4

Ingredients:

1lb. ground veal
2 tablespoons grated Parmesan cheese
1 cup tomato sauce, no sugar added
½ teaspoon garlic powder
1 teaspoon dried basil

½ teaspoon dried oregano
Salt and pepper, to taste
4 slices Provolone cheese
4 leaves Romaine lettuce
4 low-carb burger buns, toasted

Directions:

In a bowl, combine the veal with grate Parmesan, tomato sauce, garlic powder, basil, and oregano. Season with salt and pepper.
Preheat grill and shape mixture into four patties.
Grill the patties for 4-6 minutes on side, depending on the thickness.
Top each patty with a slice of Provolone cheese and cook for 1 minute.
Split buns in half and toast. Place the lettuce on half the bun and top with patty, cheese side up. Sandwich with the other bun half and serve.

Nutritional Info: Per serving

Calories: 334   Cholesterol: 142mg   Protein: 18.1g
Total fat: 17.7g   Total Carbs: 4.6g

MUSTARD **B**EEF BURGERS WITH **B**ACON

Preparation time: 5 minutes   Cooking time: 15 minutes   Servings: 6

Ingredients:

1 ½ lb. ground beef
1 tablespoon mustard
2 garlic cloves, chopped
6 strips bacon
6 sliced cheddar cheese, halved

Salt and pepper, to taste
1 tablespoon coconut oil, for frying
Some coleslaw, to serve with
6 low-carb burger buns, toasted, sliced

Directions:

In a large bowl, combine the ground beef, mustard, garlic , salt, and pepper.

Mix with clean hands and cover. Give it a rest for 15 minutes.

Meanwhile, cut the rind off bacon. Preheat oven to 400F and line baking sheet with parchment paper. Arrange the bacon onto baking sheet and bake for 8 minutes. Remove and place aside.

Shape the beef mixture into eight smaller patties. Heat the coconut oil in the grill pan. Cook the patties for 4 minutes per side. Top the patties with cheddar cheese and cook for 1 minute.

Serve patties on plate. Top with baked bacon and the sliced buns on side. A nice addition is a crunchy fresh coleslaw.

Nutritional Info: Per serving

Calories: 368
Total fat: 18.8g

Cholesterol: 125mg
Total Carbs: 1.5g

Protein: 15.5g

UMAMI SLIDERS

Preparation time: 5 minutes   Cooking time: 5 minutes   Servings: 4

Ingredients:

1lb. ground beef
2 garlic cloves, minced
1 tablespoon fish sauce
½ tablespoon applesauce, unsweetened

4 tablespoons coconut oil
Salt and pepper, to taste
4 low-carb burger buns, sliced

Directions:

Heat the coconut oil in a skillet.

Add the garlic and cook for 2 minutes or until fragrant over medium heat.

In a bowl, combine the ground beef, fish sauce, applesauce, salt, and pepper. Stir in the prepared garlic and stir until blended. Form the mixture into eight sliders.

Heat some of oil in the frying pan. Cook the sliders for 2 minutes per side.

Serve sliders with sliced buns and some fresh salad.

Nutritional Info: Per serving

Calories: 333
Total fat: 20.7g

Cholesterol: 101mg
Total Carbs: 0.9g

Protein: 24.7g

SHRIMP BURGERS

Preparation time: 5 minutes   Cooking time: 10 minutes   Servings: 6

Ingredients:

1 ½ lb. peeled and deveined shrimps
2 tablespoons fresh chives, snipped
2 tablespoons fresh coriander, chopped
¼ cup celery, minced
¼ cup radishes, minced
2 garlic cloves, minced
1 egg
1 tablespoon lime juice
1 teaspoon lemon zest
4 tablespoons almond meal

Salt and pepper, to taste
4 low-carb buns, to serve with
¼ cup coconut oil

For the salsa:
¼ cup red or green bell peppers, chopped
1 avocado, peeled and diced
1 tablespoon fresh cilantro, chopped
1 tablespoon lime juice
1 tablespoon red onion, chopped
Salt and pepper, to taste

Directions:

Prepare the salsa: combine all the ingredients in a small bowl. Give it a good stir and cover. Refrigerate until ready to use.

Prepare the burgers: preheat the grill to medium-high heat. Add coconut oil.

In a bowl of food processor, combine the shrimps, chives, coriander, celery, radishes, and garlic. Pulse few times until combined.

Transfer to a bowl, and stir in remaining ingredients. Mix with clean hands. Shape the mixture into four patties.

Brush the patties with some oil and cook for 4-5 minutes per side.

Cut the buns in half. Transfer the patties onto buns, top with salsa and sandwich with remaining bun half. Serve and enjoy.

Nutritional Info: Per serving

Calories: 481   Cholesterol: 299mg   Protein: 32.7
Total fat: 30.4g   Total Carbs: 10.2g

CHIPOTLE CHICKEN AND SAUSAGE BURGERS

Preparation time: 5 minutes   Cooking time: 10 minutes   Servings: 4

Ingredients:

1lb. ground chicken, white and dark meat combined
¾ lb. Cajun sausage
1 teaspoon fresh oregano
½ teaspoon chile powder
2 teaspoons garlic powder
½ teaspoon smoked paprika
4oz. Pepper Jack cheese, sliced

Salt and pepper, to taste

For the aioli:
1 tablespoon lime juice
1 cup Greek yogurt
½ chipotle pepper in adobo, minced
Salt and pepper, to taste

Directions:

Prepare the patties: in a large bowl, combine all the ingredients.

Mix well with clean hands and shape the mixture into six patties.

Preheat the grill to medium-high. Cook the patties for 5 minutes per side.

Meanwhile, prepare the aioli: in a mini blender combine all the ingredients.

Pulse until blended through. Place aside.

Once the patties are cooked, top each with a piece of cheese. Cook for 1 minute more.

Serve the patties with burger buns. Drizzle each patty with freshly prepared aioli. Serve after.

Nutritional Info: Per serving

Calories: 289	Cholesterol: 118mg	Protein: 20.3g
Total fat: 12.6g	Total Carbs: 1,4g	

Sesame Salmon Burger

Preparation time: 5 minutes   Cooking time: 10 minutes   Servings: 4

Ingredients:

1lb. salmon fillets, skinless
1 tablespoon plum vinegar
4 tablespoons coconut oil
1 teaspoon minced ginger
2 garlic cloves, minced

¼ cup chopped chives
2 eggs
¼ cup toasted sesame seeds
1 tablespoon almond flour
Salt and pepper, to taste

Directions:

Cut the salmon into smaller pieces. Transfer in the bowl of food blender.

Add the vinegar, coconut oil, ginger, and cloves to the salmon. Buzz until blended, but not mushy.

Stir in the remaining ingredients and stir well with a wooden spoon.

Form six patties from prepared mixture. Heat some oil in large skillet.

Cook patties for 4 minutes per side.

Serve with toasted buns.

Nutritional Info: Per serving

Calories: 355	Cholesterol: 132mg	Protein: 25.6g
Total fat: 27.3g	Total Carbs: 3.2g	

Pulled Chicken Burgers

Preparation time: 5 minutes   Cooking time: 45 minutes   Servings: 2

Ingredients:

2 chicken breasts, skin on
1 teaspoon olive oil
2 teaspoons freshly squeezed lemon juice
4 tablespoons mayonnaise
4 tablespoons basil pesto

Salt and pepper, to taste
4 grilled Portobello mushrooms

Directions:

Preheat the oven to 400F.

Brush the chicken breasts with olive oil and season to taste with salt and pepper.

Transfer the chicken into baking dish and bake, uncovered for 45 minutes.

Remove the skin and shred the chicken into fine threads.

Transfer the chicken in a bowl, and combine with lemon juice, mayonnaise, and basil pesto.

Give it all a good stir and top the half mushrooms with the chicken.

Sandwich with remaining mushrooms and serve.

Nutritional Info: Per serving

Calories: 296	Cholesterol: 85mg	Protein: 20.6g
Total fat: 15.3g	Total Carbs: 8,5g	

CUBAN PORK BURGERS

Preparation time: 5 minutes	Cooking time: 20 minutes	Servings: 6

Ingredients:

1lb. ground pork or ground pork sausage
1 egg white, whisked slightly
1 cup plantain chips
1 garlic clove, minced
4 tablespoons lard
Salt and pepper, to taste

For the serving:

1 avocado, peeled, pitted and sliced
1 tablespoon liquid eyrthritol
1 teaspoon yellow mustard
Salt and pepper, to taste

Directions:

Place the plantain chips in a food blender. Pulse until you have a coarse mixture. Transfer in a bowl. Whisk egg white in a separate bowl.

Preheat oven to 350F.

Season the pork with salt and pepper and shape mixture in four patties. Place aside.

Melt the lard in a skillet. Add minced garlic and cook until fragrant.

Dip each patty in the egg white and dredge through the plantain crumbs.

Place the patties into skillet with garlic and sear on both sides. Transfer the burgers into a baking dish and continue baking for 10 minutes. Remove from the open and let it rest for 10 minutes.

Meanwhile, in a bowl, combine the eyrthritol, mustard, salt, and pepper. Add the avocado and toss to coat.

Serve patties with low-carb burger buns and avocado slices on top.

Nutritional Info: Per serving

Calories: 258	Cholesterol: 63mg	Protein: 15.1g
Total fat: 17.8g	Total Carbs: 3.1g	

Burgers with Cashew Cream

Preparation time: 10 minutes   Cooking time: 10 minutes   Servings: 6

Ingredients:

1lb. ground beef
1 teaspoon minced garlic
½ tablespoon Sriracha
¼ cup cilantro, chopped
Salt and pepper, to taste
4 leaves Iceberg lettuce

For the cashew cream:

¼ cup roasted cashews
½ tablespoon curry powder
1 ¾ tablespoons water
1 teaspoon apple cider vinegar
¾ teaspoon eyrthritol
Salt and pepper, to taste

Directions:

In a large bowl, combine the beef, garlic, Sriracha, cilantro, salt, and pepper.
Mix with clean hands and shape the prepared mixture into four patties. Poke a deep hole in each patty.
Preheat the grill: cook the patties for four minutes per side.
Prepare the cashew cream: in a food blender combine the cashew cream ingredients. Blend until smooth.
Serve patties on a lettuce and pour a cashew cream in the hole you have made. Serve.

Nutritional Info: Per serving

Calories: 178   Cholesterol: 68mg   Protein: 13.9g
Total fat: 9.4g   Total Carbs: 2.7g

Teriyaki Turkey Burgers

Preparation time: 5 minutes   Cooking time: 10 minutes   Servings: 4

Ingredients:

1lb. ground turkey
1 cup grated zucchinis
3 garlic cloves, minced
1 tablespoon Erythritol
1 teaspoon minced fresh ginger
1 tablespoon fresh pineapple juice

¼ cup coconut oil
1 tablespoon almond flour
1 tablespoon Tamari sauce
Salt and pepper, to taste
4 low-carb burger buns

Directions:

Squeeze the grated zucchinis to remove excess liquid. Place the zucchinis in a bowl.
Add the turkey, garlic, Erythritol, ginger, pineapple juice, almond flour, Tamari sauce, coconut oil, salt, and pepper. Mix with clean hands and shape the mixture into four patties.
Preheat the grill. Cook the patties for 3 minutes per side.
Serve patties with toasted buns and some fresh salsa.

Nutritional Info: Per serving

Calories: 390   Cholesterol: 116mg   Protein: 21.2g
Total fat: 29.7g   Total Carbs: 4.0g

Mexican Chicken Burgers

Preparation time: 5 minutes   Cooking time: 10 minutes   Servings: 4

Ingredients:

1lb. ground chicken meat
½ cup grated zucchini
1 egg
1 teaspoon taco seasoning
½ cup chili powder

½ cup mild salsa
4 tablespoons olive oil
Salt and pepper, to taste
4 low-carb burger buns, toasted

Directions:

Squeeze the zucchinis to remove excess liquid and place in a bowl.

Toss in the remaining ingredients and stir with clean hands.

Preheat the grill.

Shape the prepared meat mixture into four patties. Grill the patties for 5 minutes per side.

Serve with toasted buns, lime wedges, and sliced avocado.

Nutritional Info: Per serving

Calories: 366   Cholesterol: 128mg   Protein: 26.2g
Total fat: 21.3g   Total Carbs: 10.5

Mixed Burger

Preparation time: 5 minutes   Cooking time: 10 minutes   Servings: 6

Ingredients:

1 ½ lb. ground chicken
2 green onions, chopped
1/3 cup almond meal
1 jalapeno, seeded and minced
Low-carb burger buns to serve with

¼ cup cilantro, chopped
½ green bell pepper, chopped
4 tablespoons coconut oil
Salt and pepper, to taste

Directions:

Preheat the grill.

Combine all the ingredients and stir with clean hands until combined.

Form six patties from the prepared mixture.

Grill the patties for 4 minutes per side.

Serve with toasted buns.

Nutritional Info: Per serving

Calories: 329   Cholesterol: 101mg   Protein: 14.1g
Total fat: 20.1g   Total Carbs: 2.3g

THE KING BURGER

Preparation time: 5 minutes   Cooking time: 10 minutes   Servings: 4

Ingredients:

1lb. ground beef
¼ teaspoon ground ginger
4 slices bacon
Salt and pepper, to taste

1 banana, peeled and sliced
¼ cup almond butter
Low-carb burger buns, to serve with

Directions:

Preheat grill to medium-high.
In a bowl, combine the beef with salt and pepper.
Shape the beef in four patties. Grill the patties for 5 minutes per side.
Meanwhile, cook the bacon in a skillet until crispy. Place on a paper towel and crumble.
Slice the bananas and cook in the bacon fat, with ginger for 3-4 minutes.
Heat the almond butter in a microwave until tender.
Serve the patties with toasted buns. Top each patty with almond butter, banana slices and crumbled bacon.
Serve and enjoy.

Nutritional Info: Per serving

Calories: 278   Cholesterol: 108mg   Protein: 27.3g
Total fat: 10.4g   Total Carbs: 6.1g

AUSTIN BURGER

Preparation time: 5 minutes   Cooking time: 10 minutes   Servings: 4

Ingredients:

1lb. ground beef
1 teaspoon cumin
1teaspoon chipotle powder
½ teaspoon garlic powder
Salt and pepper, to taste

Low-carb buns

For the topping:
4 tablespoons mayonnaise
½ tablespoon Sriracha sauce
1 avocado, peeled and sliced

Directions:

In a bowl, combine the beef, cumin, chipotle powder, garlic, salt, and pepper.
Preheat the grill. Shape the meat mixture into four patties and grill for 5 minutes per side.
Meanwhile, in a bowl combine the mayonnaise and Sriracha until blended.
Serve patties on top of buns. Place a tablespoon of mayo on top of patty and garnish with avocado slices.
Enjoy.

Nutritional Info: Per serving

Calories: 379   Cholesterol: 105mg   Protein: 25.6g
Total fat: 21.9g   Total Carbs: 8.3g

CAJUN BURGERS

Preparation time: 5 minutes   Cooking time: 10 minutes   Servings: 4

Ingredients:

1lb. ground beef
2 teaspoons onion powder
1 teaspoon garlic powder

2 tablespoons Cajun seasoning
Salt and pepper, to taste
4 low-carb burger buns

Directions:

In a bowl, combine all the ingredients.
Shape mixture in four patties.
Preheat the grill.
Cook the patties for 5 minutes per side.
Serve immediately, with the buns and favorite sauce.

Nutritional Info: Per serving

Calories: 217   Cholesterol: 101mg   Protein: 24.7g
Total fat: 8.1g   Total Carbs: 1,5g

AVOCADO STUFFED BURGERS

Preparation time: 5 minutes   Cooking time: 10 minutes   Servings: 8

Ingredients:

2lb. ground beef
2 garlic cloves, minced
2 tablespoons fresh cilantro, chopped
1 teaspoon dried sage, chopped
2 tablespoons Herbs de Provence
2 eggs
¼ cup coconut oil

Salt and pepper, to taste

For the spicy filling:
2 avocados, mashed
4 tablespoon mayonnaise
1 teaspoon chipotle powder
Salt and pepper, to taste

Directions:

In a large bowl, combine the beef, garlic, cilantro, sage, Herbs de Provence, eggs, salt, and pepper.
Shape mixture in 16 patties. Place aside.
In a small bowl, mash the avocado with chipotle powder, salt, and pepper.
Divide the avocado mix between 8 patties. Top with remaining six patties and pinch edges to seal.
Preheat grill to medium-high. Heat the oil. Grill the patties for 5-6 minutes per side.
Serve while still hot with toasted buns.

Nutritional Info: Per serving

Calories: 418   Cholesterol: 144mg   Protein: 26.9g
Total fat: 27.2g   Total Carbs: 6.5g

MEDITERRANEAN BURGER

Preparation time: 5 minutes + inactive time
Cooking time: 10 minutes

Servings: 4

Ingredients:

1lb. ground lamb
1 teaspoon fresh oregano, chopped
1 teaspoon fresh sage, chopped
2 garlic cloves, minced
1 tablespoon lime juice

2 tablespoon olive oil
Salt and pepper, to taste
4 low-carb burger buns
4 leaves lettuce

Directions:

In a large bowl, combine the lamb, oregano, sage, garlic, lemon juice, olive oil, salt, and pepper.
Mix with clean hands and cover. Place aside for 20 minutes. Preheat the grill to medium-high.
Shape the lamb mixture into four patties. Grill the patties for 4 minutes per side.
Serve grilled patties with buns and lettuce.
Enjoy.

Nutritional Info: Per serving

Calories: 275
Total fat: 15.4g

Cholesterol: 102mg
Total Carbs: 0.8g

Protein: 22.0g

GAME BURGERS

Preparation time: 5 minutes + inactive time
Cooking time: 10 minutes
Servings: 4

Ingredients:

1lb. ground game meat
1 teaspoon fresh basil, chopped
1 teaspoon fresh sage, chopped
4 garlic cloves, minced

3 tablespoons olive oil
Salt and pepper, to taste
4 low-carb burger buns
1 avocado, peeled and sliced

Directions:

In a bowl, combine the meat with basil, sage, garlic, oil, salt, and pepper.
Mix with clean hands and chill for 20 minutes. Preheat the grill.
Shape the game meat into four patties, around 1-inch thick.
Grill the patties for 6 minutes per side.
Slice the avocado and toast the buns.
Serve grilled patties with buns, topped with sliced avocado.
Enjoy.

Nutritional Info: Per serving

Calories: 290
Total fat: 19.2g

Cholesterol: 117mg
Total Carbs: 1.1g

Protein: 17.8g

ULTIMATE SALMON BURGER

Preparation time: 5 minutes + inactive time
Cooking time: 15 minutes

Servings: 4

Ingredients:

1lb. skinless salmon fillets, chopped
1 ½ tablespoons fish sauce
2 garlic cloves, minced
1 ½ tablespoons hot sauce
¾ tablespoon minced ginger
½ cup mayonnaise
1 tablespoon fresh lime juice

1 tablespoon fresh lemon juice
¼ cup chopped cilantro
¼ cup chopped mint
1 cup almond flour
Salt and pepper, to taste
4 low-carb burger buns

Directions:

Place the chopped salmon in a food blender. Toss in the fish sauce, garlic, hot sauce, ginger, lemon, and lime juice. Process until blended. Transfer the mixture in a bowl and stir in the mayonnaise, cilantro, mint, ¾ cups almond flour, salt, and pepper. Shape the mixture into four patties. Cover and refrigerate for 2 hours. Heat some oil in large skillet. Pat the remaining almond flour onto prepared patties.
Cook the patties for 6-7 minutes per side. Serve with toasted buns and some hot sauce.

Nutritional Info: Per serving

Calories: 317
Total fat: 22.7g

Cholesterol: 58mg
Total Carbs: 9.7g

Protein: 22.6g

CHUCK BURGERS

Preparation time: 5 minutes

Cooking time: 15 minutes

Servings: 4

Ingredients:

1lb. ground chuck
1 teaspoon Worcestershire sauce
2 tablespoon butter
Salt and pepper, to taste

1 avocado, peeled and sliced
½ tablespoon mustard
2 tablespoon mayonnaise
½ head Iceberg salad

Directions:

In a bowl, combine the ground chuck with Worcestershire sauce, salt, and pepper.
Shape the mixture into four patties.
Melt the butter in a skillet. Cook patties for until done, for 4 minutes per side.
Meanwhile, in a small bowl, combine the mustard, mayonnaise, and season to taste.
Use the lettuce as a bun. Use 2 salad leaves per patty. Place the patty on top of the lettuce. Top with avocado slices and mayonnaise mixture. Wrap the salad tightly around the patties and serve.

Nutritional Info: Per serving

Calories: 255
Total fat: 22.5g

Cholesterol: 39mg
Total Carbs: 6.8g

Protein: 7.9g

HEART BURGERS

Preparation time: 5 minutes   Cooking time: 15 minutes   Servings: 4

Ingredients:

¼ lb. ground beef heart
¾ lb. ground beef
¼ cup chopped flat-leaf parsley

4 slices Cheddar cheese
4 slices Romaine lettuce
Salt and pepper, to taste

Directions:

In a bowl, combine the ground heart, ground beef, parsley, salt, and pepper.
Shape the mixture into four patties. Preheat the grill.
Grill the patties for 3 minutes per side.
Top each patty with a cheese slice and cook for 1 minute.
Serve with lettuce instead buns.

Nutritional Info: Per serving

Calories: 319   Cholesterol: 166mg   Protein: 21.0g
Total fat: 15.9g   Total Carbs: 0.6g

SALMON AND CRAB BURGER

Preparation time: 5 minutes   Cooking time: 15 minutes   Servings: 6

Ingredients:

16oz. crabmeat
¾ lb. salmon fillets, skinless, chopped
1 egg
1 egg white
1 tablespoon hot sauce
2 tablespoons lemon juice
½ cup fresh basil, chopped
2 garlic cloves, minced
Salt, to taste

Salt and pepper, to taste
6 low-carb burger buns

For the sauce:

4 tablespoons mustard
8 tablespoons mayonnaise
½ teaspoon horseradish
1 tablespoon lemon juice

Directions:

Prepare the sauce: in a bowl, combine all the ingredients. Stir well and place aside.
Prepare the burgers: place the salmon in a food blender. Add the crabmeat and pulse few times. Transfer the salmon mix in a bowl and add the egg, egg white, hot sauce, lemon juice, basil, garlic, salt, and pepper.
Mix with clean hands and shape the mixture into four patties.
Heat some olive oil in a large frying pan. Cook the patties for 5 minutes per side.
Once done, serve with buns and prepared sauce on top.

Nutritional Info: Per serving

Calories: 275   Cholesterol: 72mg   Protein: 20.0g
Total fat: 13.4g   Total Carbs: 7.9g

BACON-CHICKEN BURGERS

Preparation time: 5 minutes   Cooking time: 15 minutes   Servings: 6

Ingredients:

1lb. ground chicken
½ cup almond meal
4 tablespoons olive oil
5 bacon slices, chopped
2 eggs

2 garlic cloves, minced
2 tablespoons chives
1 teaspoon curry, mild
Fresh ground salt and pepper

Directions:

Place chicken breasts, bacon, 1 tablespoon olive oil, and spices into food processor.

Pulse until you have smooth mixture.

Transfer to a medium bowl and add eggs, almond meal, and chives. Mix with hands or with a metal spoon until well combined.

Form patties from the mixture.

Heat remaining oil in large, non-stick skillet and add prepared patties.

Cook for 5 minutes or until golden on each side.

Serve with fresh salad or onion slices.

Nutritional Info: Per serving

Calories: 322
Total fat: 22.6g

Cholesterol: 128mg
Total Carbs: 2.5g

Protein: 22.5g

FETA CHEESE BURGERS

Preparation time: 5 minutes   Cooking time: 15 minutes   Servings: 6

Ingredients:

1lb ground beef
4 oz. feta cheese, crumbled
2 teaspoons dried parsley
1 teaspoon dried basil

2 oz. thick yogurt
1 teaspoon garlic powder
Some olive oil – for frying

Directions:

Place all ingredients in a large bowl.

Stir well with metal spoon or mix with hands, until well combined.

Form patties from the mixture and heat olive oil in large non-stick skillet.

Fry patties for 5-7 minutes or until browned,

Serve immediately with salad instead of buns.

Nutritional Info: Per serving

Calories: 199
Total fat: 8.8g

Cholesterol: 85mg
Total Carbs: 1,8g

Protein: 12.6g

Asian Style Burgers

Preparation time: 5 minutes   Cooking time: 15 minutes   Servings: 4

Ingredients:

½ lb. ground pork
½ lb. ground beef
2 tablespoons chopped cilantro
2 garlic cloves, minced
2 tablespoons fish sauce

2 tablespoons coconut aminos
2 teaspoons minced ginger
1 tablespoon chopped parsley
1 lime juiced and zested
3 tablespoons bacon fat

Directions:

In a large bowl, combine all the ingredients.

Form four patties from the prepared mixture.

Heat some bacon fat, lard or whatever you like in the large skillet.

Cook the patties for 4 minutes per side.

Serve while still hot with toasted low-carb buns.

Nutritional Info: Per serving

Calories: 282   Cholesterol: 101mg   Protein: 23.7g
Total fat: 15.2   Total Carbs: 1.6g

Spicy Lamb-Jalapeno burgers with Bacon

Preparation time: 5 minutes   Cooking time: 15 minutes   Servings: 4

Ingredients:

1 lb. grass-fed ground lamb
1 jalapeno pepper, minced
1 teaspoon smoked paprika
Sea salt to taste

1 teaspoon ground cumin
1 teaspoon dried thyme
5 strips bacon, cooked and chopped
4 tablespoons olive oil

Directions:

Place all ingredient into mixing bowl.

Mix well with hands, until thoroughly combined.

Preheat skillet and add oil.

Form burgers from prepared mixture and cook the burgers for 3-4 minutes.

Flip burgers to other side and cook until done.

Serve on plate with toasted buns and sprinkle with some fresh parsley.

Nutritional Info: Per serving

Calories: 465   Cholesterol: 128mg   Protein: 25.9g
Total fat: 32.4g   Total Carbs: 1,2g

TURKEY AND CHERRY BURGERS

Preparation time: 5 minutes + inactive time   Servings: 4
Cooking time: 15 minutes

Ingredients:

1lb. ground turkey meat
¼ cup dried cherries, unsweetened
½ teaspoon garlic powder
½ teaspoon onion powder

¼ teaspoon smoked paprika
4 slices goats cheese
Salt and pepper, to taste
4 low-carb burger buns

Directions:

Place the turkey in a bowl. Sprinkle with garlic powder, onion powder, smoked paprika, salt, and pepper. Add the cherries and stir to combine. Shape the mixture into four patties and refrigerate for 15 minutes. Preheat the grill. Cook the patties for 4 minutes per side. Top each patty with a cheese slice and cook for 1 minute more. Serve while still hot with toasted buns.

Nutritional Info: Per serving

Calories: 335   Cholesterol: 116mg   Protein: 22.0g
Total fat: 15.8g   Total Carbs: 4.0g

WASABI SALMON BURGERS

Preparation time: 5 minutes   Cooking time: 15 minutes   Servings: 4

Ingredients:

1lb. salmon fillets, skinless and chopped
4 tablespoons wasabi powder
1 tablespoon minced fresh ginger
2 tablespoons olive oil
¼ cup chopped cilantro
½ cup almond meal

1 tablespoon lime juice
2 eggs
Salt and pepper, to taste
4 low-carb burger buns, toasted, to serve with

Directions:

Combine the wasabi powder and oil to form a paste. Place the salmon in a food blender. Pulse few times and transfer into a bowl. Add the remaining ingredients, and stir well.
Shape the mixture into 1-inch thick patties. Meanwhile, heat some olive oil in a skillet.
Cook patties for 7-8 minutes per side or until golden.
Serve with toasted buns and enjoy.

Nutritional Info: Per serving

Calories: 345   Cholesterol: 132mg   Protein: 25.4g
Total fat: 22.2g   Total Carbs: 6,7g

CHUNKY AVOCADO TURKEY BURGERS

Preparation time: 5 minutes   Cooking time: 15 minutes   Servings: 4

Ingredients:

1lb. ground chicken
2 avocados, peeled, cut into chunks
1/3 cup almond meal
2 garlic cloves, finely chopped

¼ teaspoon red pepper flakes
Salt and pepper, to taste
Low-carb burger buns, to serve with

Directions:

Combine the turkey with remaining ingredients in a bowl.
Shape the mixture in a four patties.
Preheat the grill and brush with some cooking oil.
Grill the burger for 4 minutes per side.
Serve while still hot, with toasted burger buns.

Nutritional Info: Per serving

Calories: 469   Cholesterol: 101mg   Protein: 30.6g
Total fat: 32.0g   Total Carbs: 10.7g

CHINESE CHICKEN BURGER

Preparation time: 5 minutes   Cooking time: 15 minutes   Servings: 4

Ingredients:

1lb. ground chicken meat
1 tablespoon minced ginger
1 tablespoon coconut aminos
2 garlic cloves, minced
2 tablespoons softened butter

1 teaspoon Sriracha
1 scallion, minced
1 tablespoon chopped cilantro
Low-carb burger Buns
Some fresh salad, to serve with

Directions:

In a large bowl, combine the chicken with remaining ingredients.
Mix with clean hands until blended.
Heat some vegetable oil in the skillet.
Cook the patties for 6-7 minutes or until golden brown.
Serve with toasted buns and fresh salad.

Nutritional Info: Per serving

Calories: 232   Cholesterol: 103mg   Protein: 23.2g
Total fat: 9.4g   Total Carbs: 2.0g

RANCH PORK BURGERS

Preparation time: 5 minutes   Cooking time: 15 minutes   Servings: 4

Ingredients:

1 lb. ground pork
2 tablespoons lard or bacon fat
2 eggs
¼ teaspoon salt
¼ teaspoon black pepper
¼ teaspoon dried dill weed

½ teaspoon garlic powder
½ teaspoon onion powder
¼ teaspoon onion flakes
1 tablespoon fresh chopped chives
2 tablespoons chopped parsley
4 low-carb burger buns, toasted

Directions:

In a bowl, combine all the ingredients.
Mix well with clean hands until all is blended.
Heat 1-inch oil in a skillet.
Shape the pork mixture in a four patties.
Cook the patties for 6 minutes per side. Serve immediately with toasted buns and favorite sauce.

Nutritional Info: Per serving

Calories: 487   Cholesterol: 273g   Protein: 35.9g
Total fat: 21.9g   Total Carbs: 3.0g

LOW-CARB BURGER BUNS – TO SERVE WITH

Preparation time: 5 minutes + inactive time   Servings: 4
Cooking time: 15 minutes

Ingredients:

4 tablespoons melted butter
½ cup ground flaxseeds
½ cup almond flour

4 eggs
2 teaspoons baking powder
1 teaspoon salt

Directions:

Preheat oven to 375F and line baking sheet with parchment paper.
In a bowl, whisk the eggs.
In a separate bowl, combine the remaining ingredients.
Fold in the eggs and stir using a rubber spatula. Shape the dough and divide in four balls.
Transfer the balls onto baking sheet and flatten a bit.
Bake for 15-18 minutes or until inserted toothpick comes out clean.
Serve with prepared patties.

Nutritional Info: Per serving

Calories: 281   Cholesterol: 194mg   Protein: 9.8g
Total fat: 23.8g   Total Carbs: 6.0g

Keto Slow cooker recipes

SLOW COOKER CHICKEN FAJITAS

Preparation time: 5 minutes   Cooking time: 5 hours   Servings: 4

Ingredients:
1 ½ lb. chicken breasts, boneless and skinless
½ teaspoon ground coriander
1 teaspoon cumin
Fresh ground salt and pepper – to taste
1 tablespoon chopped garlic

1 teaspoon chili powder
10oz. tomatoes, peeled and pureed in food blender
2 tablespoons olive oil
½ cup shredded cheese – by your choice

Directions:
Place garlic in bottom of slow cooker. Top with chicken.
Combine spices and oil in bowl and drizzle evenly over chicken.
Add remaining ingredients and cover the slow cooker.
Cook on high for 4-5 hours.
Remove chicken and slice before serving.
Serve with low-carb tortilla and sprinkle with shredded cheese.

Nutritional Info: Per serving
Calories: 486
Total fat: 24,8g

Cholesterol: 167mg
Total Carbs: 7.4g

Protein: 37.7g

CHICKEN CHILI SOUP

Preparation time: 5 minutes   Cooking time: 6 hours   Servings: 8

Ingredients:
2 tablespoons butter, unsalted
8 slices bacon
1 red pepper, thinly sliced
1 teaspoon black pepper
1 teaspoon salt
1 tablespoon thyme
1 tablespoon minced garlic

1 cup chicken stock
3 tablespoons tomato paste
¼ cup coconut milk, unsweetened
8 boneless chicken tights
1 tablespoon coconut flour
3 tablespoons lemon juice

Directions:
Place butter in the center of slow cooker.
Place pepper in bottom of slow cooker and cover with chicken tights.
Cut bacon slices in half and cover the chicken with them.
Add seasonings and coconut flour.

Add liquids and tomato paste.

Cover and cook on low for 6 hours.

Break up the chicken before serving.

Serve with sour cream while still hot.

Nutritional Info: Per serving

Calories: 164	Cholesterol: 48mg	Protein: 11.1g
Total fat: 11.3	Total Carbs: 3.4g	

CORNED BEEF AND CABBAGE

Preparation time: 5 minutes   Cooking time: 8 hours   Servings: 10

Ingredients:

4 cups water
3 tablespoons olive oil
1 celery bunch
5 ½ lb. corned beef
1 large head cabbage
½ teaspoon black pepper

½ teaspoon salt
½ teaspoon ground coriander
½ teaspoon ground mustard
½ teaspoon all spice
½ teaspoon marjoram, ground
½ teaspoon dried thyme

Directions:

Slice the celery.

Line the bottom of slow cooker with chopped vegetables and oil.

Add water. Combine spices and herbs in small bowl.

Mix all sides of corned beef with spices, rubbing them well.

Place meat on top of vegetables and sprinkle with remaining spices, if there are any.

Cover and cook on low for 7 hours.

Discard first layer of cabbage and cut in wedges.

Rinse well under running water and set on top of meat.

Place cabbage in slow cooker, cover and cook for 1 hour additionally.

Slice beef and serve while still hot.

Nutritional Info: Per serving

Calories: 492	Cholesterol: 156mg	Protein: 25.1g
Total fat: 35.6g	Total Carbs: 7.4g	

BBQ SLOW COOKER ROAST

Preparation time: 5 minutes   Cooking time: 5 hours   Servings: 8

Ingredients:

3 lb. beef chuck shoulder roast
½ teaspoon liquid smoke
2 ½ teaspoons minced garlic
2 tablespoons vinegar

3 cloves garlic, chopped
2 tablespoons Splenda
1 tablespoon Worchester sauce
1 ½ tablespoons bacon grease

½ tablespoon yellow mustard Fresh ground salt and pepper – to taste

Directions:

Coat the roast with salt and pepper.

Heat bacon fat in large skillet and brown roast all sides, over medium-high heat.

Place the meat in slow cooker and fry garlic in remaining bacon fat for 2minutes.

Stir in mustard, liquid smoke, garlic, vinegar, and Splenda and Worchester sauce.

Pour prepared sauce over roast and cover the slow cooker.

Cook meat for 75 minutes per lb. of roast or in this case for 5 hours.

Remove meat from slow cooker and separate in portions.

Serve while still hot.

Nutritional Info: Per serving

Calories: 484	Cholesterol: 207mg	Protein: 27.0g
Total fat: 19.0g	Total Carbs: 3.7g	

SLOW COOKER CHILI

Preparation time: 5 minutes Cooking time: 6 hours Servings: 8

Ingredients:

8 thick cuts bacon 1 14 oz. can diced tomatoes

2 tablespoons lard 3 oz. tomato paste

2 small green peppers Fresh ground salt and pepper – to taste

2 lb. ground pork ½ tablespoon chili seasoning

Directions:

Finely chop peppers; place the peppers in the bottom of slow cooker.

Heat large skillet with lard over medium-high heat and add ground pork.

Brown pork and season with salt and pepper; drain well and transfer into slow cooker.

Cut bacon in small, bite-size pieces and fry in skillet over medium-high heat.

Drain bacon and place in slow cooker.

Drain tomatoes and place in slow cooker.

Add seasonings and cover slow cooker.

Cook on low for 6 hours.

Nutritional Info: Per serving

Calories: 247	Cholesterol: 93mg	Protein: 13.1g
Total fat: 10.2g	Total Carbs: 4.9g	

SLOW COOKER TURKEY FAJITAS

Preparation time: 5 minutes Cooking time: 5 hours Servings: 6

Ingredients:

1 ½ lb. turkey breasts, boneless ½ teaspoon ground coriander

2 tablespoons bacon fat

1 teaspoon cumin

Fresh ground salt and pepper – to taste

1 tablespoon chopped garlic

1 teaspoon chili powder

1 can 15 oz. diced tomatoes with green chiles

½ cup shredded cheese – by your choice

Directions:

Place bacon far garlic in bottom of slow cooker. Top with turkey.

Combine spices in bowl and sprinkle evenly over turkey.

Add remaining ingredients and cover the slow cooker.

Cook on high for 4-5 hours. Remove turkey and slice before serving.

Serve with low-carb tortilla and sprinkle with shredded cheese.

Nutritional Info: Per serving

Calories: 274

Total fat: 15.2g

Cholesterol: 76mg

Total Carbs: 8.6g

Protein: 12,2g

CHICKEN SLOW COOKER CHOWDER

Preparation time: 10 minutes   Cooking time: 6 hours   Servings: 6

Ingredients:

1 lb. chicken

2 cups chicken stock, divided

1 teaspoon black pepper

1 teaspoon salt

8 oz. cream cheese

4 tablespoons butter, divided

1 onion, thinly sliced

6 oz. cremini mushrooms

2 celery stalks, chopped

1 leek, trimmed, washed and chopped; white and light green parts only

1 cup heavy cream

1 teaspoon thyme

4 garlic cloves, minced

1 lb. bacon, cooked and crumbled

Directions:

Heat slow cooker on low setting and add garlic, leek, onion, mushrooms, half of butter and half of stock.

Season with salt and pepper and cook for 1 hour, covered.

Meanwhile, heat butter in large skillet over medium-high heat.

Pan-sear chicken breasts until brown on both sides.

Remove chicken from the pan and deglaze pan with remaining chicken stock.

Using spatula scrape up any bits of chicken that may be stuck to the pan.

Add chicken stock to slow cooker.

Add heavy cream, cream cheese and thyme to slow cooker; stir well until combined.

Once chicken is cooled, cut into bite-size pieces and add to slow cooker, along with bacon.

Stir until all ingredients are combined and cover; cook on low for 6-8 hours.

Serve while still hot.

Nutritional Info: Per serving

Calories: 825

Total fat: 62.5g

Cholesterol: 231g

Total Carbs: 9.1g

Protein: 50.8g

SLOW COOKER PIZZA

Preparation time: 5 minutes   Cooking time: 6 hours   Servings: 8

Ingredients:

¾ lb. minced beef, cooked and drained
¾ lb. pork sausage, cooked
15 oz. marinara sauce
18 slices pork pepperoni

3 cups mozzarella cheese, shredded
3 cups baby spinach, raw

For topping:
1 cup pitted green olives, halved

Directions:

Combine sausage meat, minced beef and marinara in a bowl. You can do this with clean hands so flavors can blend nicely. Place half of mixture in slow cooker, preferably 6-quart. You can go with smaller, but in such case prolong end of cooking for 30 minutes, since bottom part will be thicker.
Place ½ of baby spinach on top of meat mix; top with pepperoni slices and ½ desired toppings.
Place half mozzarella and repeat layers. Cook on low setting, covered for 4-6 hours.
Cool slightly before slicing and serving.

Nutritional Info: Per serving

Calories: 363   Cholesterol: 93mg   Protein: 18.2g
Total fat: 23.5g   Total Carbs: 7.1g

KETO SLOW COOKER ITALIAN MEATBALLS

Preparation time: 5 minutes   Cooking time: 7 hours   Servings: 6

Ingredients:

2 lb. ground beef
4 tablespoons softened butter
4 garlic cloves, minced
2 eggs
1 tablespoon almond meal
1 teaspoon salt

½ teaspoon cayenne pepper
1 teaspoon oregano
1 teaspoon dried basil
Some olive oil
12oz. can tomato sauce
Additional salt and pepper

Directions:

Place meat in a large bowl. Add eggs, butter, garlic, almond meal, spices and herbs.
Stir with clean hands until combined thoroughly. Roll meat into balls, around 1 ½-inches large.
Heat some oil in large non-stick skillet and slightly brown on all sides.
Transfer meat balls in slow cooker and cook for 6 hours on low.
Add tomato sauce, season with salt and pepper; cook for 1 hour more.
Serve while still hot.

Nutritional Info: Per serving

Calories: 393   Cholesterol: 210mg   Protein: 23.9g
Total fat: 19.2   Total Carbs: 4.3g

BROCCOLI CHEESE SOUP

Preparation time: 5 minutes   Cooking time: 4 hours   Servings: 6

Ingredients:

4 cups chicken stock
4 tablespoons butter
16 oz. frozen chopped broccoli florets
8 oz. shredded cheddar cheese
½ cup chopped red bell pepper
1 ½ cups water

1 ½ cups heavy cream
¾ teaspoon salt
¼ teaspoon white pepper
2 tablespoons fresh chives, chopped
½ teaspoon dry mustard

Directions:

Heat slow cooker.

Add butter and when melted stir in broccoli and red bell pepper.

Add remaining ingredients, except chives and cheese and stir well.

Cover and cook for 3 hours on low.

Stir in heavy cream and cook for 30 minutes more.

Serve while still hot, garnished with fresh chives.

Nutritional Info: Per serving

Calories: 361   Cholesterol: 101mg   Protein: 12.9g
Total fat: 32.0g   Total Carbs: 7.8g

KETO SLOW COOKER PULLED PORK

Preparation time: 5 minutes   Cooking time: 6 hours   Servings: 8

Ingredients:

2 lb. pork shoulder
4 oz. low-carb/sugar free BBQ sauce
4oz. butter
1 cup beef stock

A dash of cinnamon
1 tablespoon chipotle sauce
2 teaspoons hot sauce

Directions:

Preheat slow cooker and set in pork meat.

Pour beef stock over meat; add cinnamon and cover.

Cook on low for 6-7 hours.

After cooking time has ended drain the slow cooker.

Add sauces, melted butter, and set aside for 30 minutes so flavors can blend.

Pull pork with forks and serve while still hot.

Nutritional Info: Per serving

Calories: 437   Cholesterol: 133mg   Protein: 26.9g
Total fat: 35.8g   Total Carbs: 1.5g

CREAMY CHICKEN KETO SOUP

Preparation time: 5 minutes   Cooking time: 8 hours   Servings: 6

Ingredients:

3 chicken breasts, cooked and shredded
4 cups chicken stock
8 oz. sliced mushrooms.
1 teaspoon thyme
2 garlic cloves, chopped

1 teaspoon parsley
1 brown onion, sliced
1 cup heavy cream
2 handfuls spinach, raw and chopped
2 celery stalks, diced

Directions:

Cook chicken breasts in pot with salted water until tender; shred finely.

Place chicken, onions, celery, parsley, mushrooms, garlic, thyme, and chicken stock into slow cooker.

Cover and cook on low for 8 hours. **30 minutes before serving stir in cream.**

Stir to combine and continue cooking until soup is heated through.

Right before serving stir in spinach and give it a good stir.

Serve while still hot.

Nutritional Info: Per serving

Calories: 206   Cholesterol: 80mg   Protein: 14.4g
Total fat: 14.2g   Total Carbs: 4.3g

KETO BACON QUICHE

Preparation time: 5 minutes   Cooking time: 5 hours   Servings: 6

Ingredients:

10 eggs, whisked
1 cup chopped onion
10 pieces of bacon
1 cup heavy cream

½ teaspoon cayenne pepper
2 cups baby spinach, fresh, stems removed
2 tablespoons butter
8 oz. shredded cheddar cheese

Directions:

Grease slow cooker with butter and turn it on low.

Add remaining butter and let it melts.

Cook the bacon in large non-stick skillet until crumbly. Drain and set aside.

Beat eggs in large bowl; whisk in cream cheese, pepper, onion and spinach.

Pour the mixture in slow cooker.

Tear the cooked bacon in ½-inch pieces and top eggs with bacon.

Cover and cook on low for 4-5 hours.

Quiche is ready when firm to the touch.

Nutritional Info: Per serving

Calories: 428   Cholesterol: 262g   Protein: 23.5g
Total fat: 35.6g   Total Carbs: 4.0g

KETO CHILI STEW

Preparation time: 5 minutes   Cooking time: 5 hours   Servings: 6

Ingredients:

0.25 lb. ground beef
½ lb. cubed beef stew meat
½ medium zucchini, chopped
1 ½ tablespoons chili powder
½ teaspoon garlic powder
1 cup organic beef stock

1 cup sliced mushrooms
¼ cup pureed pumpkin
3 garlic cloves, minced
14 oz. tomato sauce, pure
3 tablespoons lard

Directions:

Brown ground beef in skillet ad transfer into slow cooker; set on high.

Add tomato sauce, beef stock, pumpkin puree, garlic powder and half of chili powder.

Stir well.

Heat ½ tablespoon coconut oil in same skillet in which you have browned beef and cook onion, minced garlic, zucchini and mushrooms, over medium-high heat or until tender.

Transfer cooked veggies in slow cooker.

In same skillet heat remaining oil and add remaining chili powder; mix together and remove from the heat.

Add beef stew meat to the skillet and place skillet back on the heat; toss and stir meat until coated.

Add coated meat to slow cooker and cover all; cook on high for 2 hours. Reduce heat to low and cook for 4-5 hours.

Serve while still hot.

Nutritional Info: Per serving

Calories: 193
Total fat: 11.5g

Cholesterol: 57mg
Total Carbs: 5.7g

Protein: 12.4g

SLOW COOKER PIZZA WITH CAULIFLOWER CRUST

Preparation time: 15 minutes   Cooking time: 4 hours   Servings: 6

Ingredients:

1 large head cauliflower
2 eggs, whisked
¼ teaspoon salt
½ cup shredded Cheddar cheese
1 teaspoon dried basil

Topping:
1 ½ cups Italian shredded cheese blend
½ teaspoon dried rosemary
½ cup Alfredo sauce*

Directions:

Prepare the Alfredo sauce*; melt 2 tablespoons butter in sauce pan over medium heat.

Add 2 oz. cream cheese and ½ teaspoon garlic powder.

Whisk with wire until smooth.

Add ½ cup milk, little at the time, whisking to break lumps.

Stir in 1 ½ oz. grated parmesan and pinch of pepper.

Remove from the heat when sauce reaches desired consistency; set aside to cool.

Prepare the pizza; cut cauliflower in florets and place in food processor.

Pulse until you have rice size pieces.

Place in a bowl and add eggs, ½ cup cheese, salt and basil; mix together well.

Transfer mix to slow cooker, coated with oil and press with spatula or hands to make a crust.

Top with Alfredo sauce, cheese and sprinkle with rosemary.

Cover but prop lid with wooden spoon handle.

Cook on high for 2-4 hours, depending on crust thickness.

Cooked crust need to have slightly browned edges.

Turn off heat and let pizza stand for 30 minutes in crock pot before slicing and serving.

Nutritional Info: Per serving

Calories: 184	Cholesterol: 94mg	Protein: 12.1g
Total fat: 14.2g	Total Carbs: 3.0g	

KETO CLAM CHOWDER

Preparation time: 5 minutes	Cooking time: 6 hours	Servings: 6

Ingredients:

1 cup clam juice

¾ cup heavy cream

1 tablespoon butter

1 teaspoon sea salt

2 tablespoons chicken stock

1 small shallot, thinly sliced

2 garlic cloves, minced

1 15 oz. can whole baby clams, drained

½ lb. thick cut bacon

1 celery rib, chopped

½ teaspoon black pepper

4 oz. cream cheese, softened

½ teaspoon thyme

Directions:

Heat slow cooker on low heat.

Add garlic, chicken stock, celery, shallot, onion, butter, salt and pepper in slow cooker.

Cover and cook vegetables for 50 minutes on low.

Add bacon, clams and clam juice into slow cooker; stir to combine.

Add cream cheese, heavy cream and thyme.

Mix until there are no lumps and all ingredients are well blended.

Cover and cook for 6-8 hours.

Serve while still hot.

Nutritional Info: Per serving

Calories: 395	Cholesterol: 88mg	Protein: 16.5g
Total fat: 30.1g	Total Carbs: 13.2g	

SLOW COOKER PORK RIBS

Preparation time: 5 minutes   Cooking time: 8 hours   Servings: 6

Ingredients:
3 lb. pork ribs   2 scallions, thinly chopped
½ cup water   1-inch ginger, thinly sliced
¼ cup soy sauce   2 tablespoon olive or coconut oil

Directions:
Place scallions, and ginger in bottom of slow cooker, with olive oil. Toss to coat.
Add pork ribs and pour over water and soy sauce.
Cover and cook on low for 8 hours.
Serve while still hot.

Nutritional Info: Per serving
Calories: 630   Cholesterol: 234mg   Protein: 40.6g
Total fat: 40.5g   Total Carbs: 1.4g

SLOW COOKER PORK CARNITAS

Preparation time: 5 minutes   Cooking time: 4 hours   Servings: 8

Ingredients:
4 lb. Boston pork butt   ½ tablespoon pepper
½ cup water   2 tablespoons minced garlic
1 tablespoon thyme   1 tablespoon bacon grease
1 tablespoon chili powder   1 tablespoon cumin
½ tablespoon salt

Directions:
Rub the slow cooker with bacon grease.
Add the garlic.
Remove most of fat from fatty part of pork and make a crisscross pattern on meat.
Mix spices and herbs in meat and if there are remaining spices sprinkle over onions.
Place meat in slow cooker and pour over water.
Cook on high for 4 hours, or 1 hour per lb.
Done meat should fall apart.
Serve while still hot.

Nutritional Info: Per serving
Calories: 449   Cholesterol: 209mg   Protein: 51.0g
Total fat: 15.5g   Total Carbs: 2.0g

SLOW COOKER CARNE ASADA

Preparation time: 15 minutes   Cooking time: 5 hours   Servings: 4

Ingredients:

2 lb. chuck roast
¼ cup extra-virgin olive oil
1 teaspoon red pepper flakes
2 teaspoons oregano
1 shallot, chopped

Juice of 2 limes
¼ cup chopped cilantro
½ teaspoons coriander
2 teaspoon salt
4 garlic cloves, minced

Directions:

Rinse chuck roast and pat dry with kitchen towels.
Set aside for 30 minutes.
Place all remaining ingredients in food processor and pulse until thoroughly combined.
Place chock roast in slow cooker and cover with prepared asada marinade.
Add ¼ cup water and cover; cook on high for 5 hours.
Remove meat from slow cooker and let it stand for 20 minutes.
Slice meat across grain and serve while still hot.

Nutritional Info: Per serving

Calories: 606   Cholesterol: 229mg   Protein: 45.5g
Total fat: 31.6g   Total Carbs: 1.8g

SPICY TOMATO PORK

Preparation time: 5 minutes   Cooking time: 6 hours   Servings: 4

Ingredients:

2 lb. pork tenderloin, cut into 1-inch pieces
2 tablespoons olive oil
4 jalapeno pepper, diced
2 teaspoons ground cumin
4 garlic cloves, crushed

8 oz. mushrooms, quartered
4 garlic cloves, crushed
2 teaspoons sea salt
2 teaspoon black pepper
1 yellow bell pepper, seeded and chopped

Directions:

Heat oil in large skillet over medium-high heat.
Season the pork with garlic and pepper; add pork to skillet and brown all sides.
Place peppers, mushrooms and garlic in pan and cook until tender.
Add all to slow cooker and sprinkle with cumin.
Cover and cook for 6 hours or until pork is tender.

Nutritional Info: Per serving

Calories: 341   Cholesterol: 166mg   Protein: 42.3g
Total fat: 16.6g   Total Carbs: 8.1g

SLOW COOKER SAUSAGES AND PEPPERS

Preparation time: 5 minutes　　　　Cooking time: 6 hours　　　　Servings: 4

Ingredients:

8 Italian sausages
1 jar marinara sauce; without sugar

1 green bell peppers, sliced

Directions:

Place peppers in bottom of slow cooker. Add sausages and cover.
Cook on low for 6 hours. Serve while still hot.

Nutritional Info: Per serving

Calories: 300　　　　　　Cholesterol: 64mg　　　　　　Protein: 15.7g
Total fat: 22.3g　　　　　Total Carbs: 8.8g

KETO CHILI VERDE

Preparation time: 5 minutes　　　　Cooking time: 8 hours　　　　Servings: 6

Ingredients:

2 lb. pork, country style ribs
10 oz. green salsa
1 teaspoon cumin

2 garlic cloves, minced
2 teaspoons chili powder

Directions:

Rub pork with chili and cumin and set aside for 2 hours.
Place pork in slow cooker and add remaining spices, if there are any left.
Place in garlic. Top all with salsa and cover with lid.
Cook for 7-8 hours on low.
Enjoy with shredded cheese.

Nutritional Info: Per serving

Calories: 237　　　　　　Cholesterol: 110mg　　　　　　Protein: 30.0g
Total fat: 7.1g　　　　　Total Carbs: 3.2g

KETO TOMATO CHOWDER

Preparation time: 15 minutes　　　　Cooking time: 8 hours　　　　Servings: 4

Ingredients:

28 oz. tomatoes, boiled for 1 minutes and
peeled
1.5 cups heavy cream
2 celery stalks, chopped
2 cups shredded cabbage

1 teaspoon fresh ground pepper
4 cups chicken stock
½ cup grated parmesan
1 bunch celery, chopped
½ cup basil

Directions:

Make small cross on bottom of tomatoes and place in boiling water. Cook for 1 minutes and peel the skin off, cut off the hard parts; place tomatoes in food blender and process until smooth.

Place all ingredients, except parmesan and heavy cream in slow cooker and cook on low for 8 hours.

Turn off heat and using immersion blender puree until smooth.

Stir in heavy cream and parmesan cheese. Serve immediately.

Nutritional Info: Per serving

Calories: 206

Total fat: 17.1g

Cholesterol: 55mg

Total Carbs: 8.0g

Protein: 9.1g

CREAMY MUSHROOM AND FENNEL SOUP

Preparation time: 5 minutes   Cooking time: 8 hours   Servings: 4

Ingredients:

1 cup chicken stock

5 oz. mushrooms

½ shallot, chopped

½ leek, chopped

1 tablespoon butter

2 cups water

½ fennel bulb

2 tablespoons dry sherry

1 cup heavy cream

½ teaspoon red pepper flakes

Small pinch salt

Small pinch pepper

Directions:

Melt butter in large skillet and add shallot and leek; cook over medium-high heat for 5 minutes.

Slice the mushrooms and add into skillet; cook until golden brown.

Transfer mixture into slow cooker and stir in stock, chopped fennel bulb, dry sherry, and water.

Season with salt and pepper and add red pepper flakes.

Cover and cook on low for 7-8 hours.

Turn off the crock pot and puree with immersion blender.

Stir in heavy cream and serve soup warm.

Nutritional Info: Per serving

Calories: 156

Total fat: 14.3g

Cholesterol: 49mg

Total Carbs: 6.0g

Protein: 2.5g

SLOW COOKER SARDINES

Preparation time: 5 minutes   Cooking time: 8 hours   Servings: 4

Ingredients:

1 lb. sardines, cut into small pieces, or if really small cut in half

½ cup tomato puree

4 tablespoon olive oil, cooking

1 cup onions, chopped

2 tomatoes, diced, core removed

2 garlic cloves, chopped

Fresh ground salt and pepper

½ teaspoon cayenne pepper

¼ teaspoon hot sauce

Directions:

Drizzle olive oil in bottom of slow cooker.
Place sardines and top with onions and garlic.
Add tomato slices, tomato puree and hot sauce.
Add seasoning and cover.
Cook on low for 8 hours.
Serve while still hot.

Nutritional Info: Per serving

Calories: 393	Cholesterol: 161mg	Protein: 26.4g
Total fat: 27.3g	Total Carbs: 8.5g	

Slow cooker zucchini Bolognese

Preparation time: 5 minutes	Cooking time: 4 hours	Servings: 4

Ingredients:

For the pasta:
5 large zucchinis, cut with veggie spiral cutter, to make spaghettis

For the sauce:
1 head cauliflower, cut into florets
2 garlic cloves, minced

½ cup vegetable stock
¼ teaspoon red pepper flakes
16oz. diced tomatoes
Fresh ground pepper
2 teaspoon dried oregano
½ cup butter

Directions:

Place all sauce ingredients in slow cooker.
Cover and cook on high for 3 ½ hours.
Mash cauliflower with fork until breaks in small parts.
Serve with zucchini noodles.

Nutritional Info: Per serving

Calories: 245	Cholesterol: 61mg	Protein: 2.7g
Total fat: 23.4g	Total Carbs: 9.0g	

Stuffed peppers

Preparation time: 5 minutes	Cooking time: 6 hours	Servings: 6

Ingredients:

4 bell peppers, red or yellow
1 lb. ground Italian sausage
2 teaspoons dried basil
2 teaspoons dried thyme
2 teaspoons dried oregano

4 oz. tomato paste
1 teaspoon garlic, minced
1 onion, chopped
½ head cauliflower, chopped to get rice consistency

Directions:

Cut tops of peppers and scoop out the seeds; reserve tops.
Combine chopped cauliflower with minced garlic, onion and dried herbs.
Combine until blended.
Heat large skillet and brown sausage over medium-high heat.
Combine sausage and tomato paste with cauliflower mix.
Fill peppers with prepared mix and arrange in slightly oiled slow cooker.
Place tops on peppers and cover the slow cooker.
Cook on low for 6 hours.
Serve while still hot.

Nutritional Info: Per serving

Calories: 308	Cholesterol: 64mg	Protein: 16.6g
Total fat: 22.8g	Total Carbs: 11.0g	

Pizza chicken

Preparation time: 5 minutes	Cooking time: 4 hours	Servings: 4

Ingredients:

4 boneless and skinless chicken fillets
20 pepperoni slices
1.5 cups marinara sauce, without sugar

1 cup grated Parmesan cheese
1/2 cup heavy cream
Fresh ground salt and pepper

Directions:

Place marinara sauce and heavy cream in bottom of slow cooker appliance.
Add chicken and season with salt and pepper.
Lay pepperoni over chicken and cover with lid.
Cook on low for 4 hours.
Turn off slow cooker and add in grated cheese.
Place the lid back on and cook until cheese is melted.
Serve while still hot.

Nutritional Info: Per serving

Calories: 514	Cholesterol: 133mg	Protein: 31.0g
Total fat: 30.2g	Total Carbs: 16.8g	

Wrapped Italian chicken

Preparation time: 5 minutes	Cooking time: 4 hours	Servings: 4

Ingredients:

4 boneless, skinless chicken tights
1 cup marinara sauce, without sugar
4 pieces bacon
4 oz. button mushrooms

2 tablespoons butter
1 teaspoon Italian seasoning

Directions:

Wrap each piece of chicken with bacon and secure with toothpicks.
Set in bottom of slow cooker greased with butter.
Pour over marinara sauce and sprinkle with Italian seasoning.
Cover and cook on low for 4 hours.
Serve immediately.

Nutritional Info: Per serving

Calories: 259   Cholesterol: 81mg   Protein: 24.1g
Total fat: 14.4g   Total Carbs: 8.6g

PROTEIN: ZUCCHINI KETO SOUP

Preparation time: 5 minutes   Cooking time: 5 hours   Servings: 4

Ingredients:

2 cups vegetable stock   ¼ teaspoon salt
1 tablespoon butter   ¼ teaspoon pepper
4 cups chopped green zucchinis   1 cup heavy cream

Directions:

Combine all ingredients in slow cooker, except heavy cream.
Cook for 5 hours on low or until zucchini is tender.
Turn off slow cooker and puree soup with immersion blender.
Stir in heavy cream and serve.

Nutritional Info: Per serving

Calories: 147   Cholesterol: 49mg   Protein: 2.0g
Total fat: 14.2g   Total Carbs: 4.7g

Pressure Keto recipes

PORK, BACON AND KALE

Preparation time: 5 minutes | Cooking time: 30 minutes | Servings: 4

Ingredients:

2oz. chopped bacon
1lb. ground pork
2 garlic cloves, minced
1 teaspoon crushed dried oregano
4 cups chicken broth

12oz. coconut milk
2 tablespoons sesame seeds flour
2 cups copped kale
2 cups chopped cauliflower
Salt and pepper, to taste

Directions:

Cook the bacon in skillet until crunchy. Crumble and place aside. Reserve some of the bacon fat.
Heat bacon fat in the pressure cooker. Add the garlic and cook until fragrant. Add the pork and cook until browned. Add broth, kale, and cauliflower. Season to taste.
Whisk the sesame seeds flour and coconut milk. Pour the mixture into pressure cooker and lock the lid.
Bring the pressure to high and maintain the pressure for 20 minutes.
Use a quick pressure release and open the lid. Serve while still hot.

Nutritional Info: Per serving

Calories: 488 | Cholesterol: 98mg | Protein: 32.4g
Total fat: 31.6g | Total Carbs: 9.0g

BEEF STEAK WITH PEPPERS

Preparation time: 5 minutes | Cooking time: 20 minutes | Servings: 4

Ingredients:

2lb. round beef steak
4 tablespoons olive oil
14oz. beef broth

2 green bell peppers, sliced
1 teaspoon red pepper flakes
Salt and pepper, to taste

Directions:

Season the steak with salt and pepper. Heat oil in a pressure cooker and brown the steak.
Add the remaining ingredients and lock the lid.
Bring the pressure to high and reduce to medium. Maintain the pressure for 15 minutes.
Release pressure naturally and open the lid.
Serve and enjoy.

Nutritional Info: Per serving

Calories: 578 | Cholesterol: 203mg | Protein: 41.5g
Total fat: 28.9g | Total Carbs: 5.1g

Sausage and Duck stew

Preparation time: 5 minutes   Cooking time: 40 minutes   Servings: 6

Ingredients:

2lb. duck legs, boneless, cut into smaller pieces
4 tablespoons butter
1 tablespoon olive oil
4 garlic cloves, minced
2 celery ribs, chopped

14oz. pork liverwurst
5 cups chicken broth
3 cups mushrooms, sliced
1 teaspoon dried thyme
Salt and pepper, to taste

Directions:

Heat olive oil and butter in a pressure cooker.
Cook the garlic until fragrant. Toss in the duck and cook until browned.
Add the remaining ingredients and stir gently.
Lock the lid and bring the pressure to high. Maintain the pressure for 40 minutes.
Use a natural pressure release method.
Open the lid and serve while still hot.

Nutritional Info: Per serving

Calories: 624
Total fat: 39.0g

Cholesterol: 230mg
Total Carbs: 2.6g

Protein: 42.6g

Citrus Mackerel

Preparation time: 5 minutes   Cooking time: 10 minutes   Servings: 4

Ingredients:

16oz. mackerel
2 tablespoons olive oil
Juice and zest from 1 lemon

1-inch piece of ginger
1 cup fish stock
Salt and pepper, to taste

Directions:

Brush the fish with olive oil and season to taste.
Pour the fish stock into pressure cooker. Add the ginger.
Arrange the fish onto steaming basket and place into pressure cooker.
Close the cooker and bring the pressure to high.
Maintain the pressure for 7 minutes.
Meanwhile combine the lemon zest and juice.
Use a quick pressure release and open the cooker.
Serve fish with prepared lemon sauce.

Nutritional Info: Per serving

Calories: 367
Total fat: 27.7g

Cholesterol: 86mg
Total Carbs: 1.2g

Protein: 28.4g

CHICKEN SOUP

Preparation time: 5 minutes   Cooking time: 15 minutes   Servings: 4

Ingredients:

4oz. boneless, skinless chicken breasts
3 cups homemade chicken broth
½ cup chopped celery
2 garlic cloves, minced

2 tablespoons ghee
¼ cup hot sauce
1 cup heavy cream
1 cup shredded Cheddar cheese

Directions:

In a pressure cooker, combine the chicken, broth, celery, garlic, ghee, and the hot sauce.
Lock the lid and bring to the high pressure. Maintain the pressure for 10 minutes.
Use a quick-pressure release method and unlock the lid.
Shred the chicken and stir in the heavy cream and cheese.
Serve while still hot.

Nutritional Info: Per serving

Calories: 362   Cholesterol: 112mg   Protein: 19.8g
Total fat: 30.0g   Total Carbs: 3.0g

CREAMY CHICKEN AND MUSHROOMS

Preparation time: 5 minutes   Cooking time: 15 minutes   Servings: 4

Ingredients:

2 tablespoons butter, melted
2 garlic cloves, minced
1lb. chicken breasts, cut into small slices
2oz. mushrooms, sliced
6oz. chicken stock

4oz. heavy cream
½ cup water
½ teaspoon basil
Salt and pepper, to taste

Directions:

Combine the butter, garlic and sliced mushrooms into a pressure cooker.
Select the saute button and cook the mushrooms until soft.
Add the remaining ingredients and give it a good stir.
Lock the lid and bring the pressure to high. Maintain the pressure for 15 minutes.
Use a natural pressure release method. Serve while still hot.

Nutritional Info: Per serving

Calories: 371   Cholesterol: 155mg   Protein: 24.1g
Total fat: 24.8g   Total Carbs: 1.9g

SIMPLE CHICKEN

Preparation time: 5 minutes   Cooking time: 20 minutes   Servings: 4

Ingredients:

4lb. chicken legs
½ cup tamari soy sauce
½ cup white wine vinegar

1 teaspoon black peppercorns
2 bay leaves
2 whole garlic cloves

Directions:

Set the pressure cooker to medium.

Add all the ingredients into the pressure cooker.

Bring the pressure to high and maintain the pressure for 20 minutes.

Use a quick pressure release method. Open the lid and discard the bay leaves.

Serve after.

Nutritional Info: Per serving

Calories: 891   Cholesterol: 304mg   Protein: 67.1g
Total fat: 33.7g   Total Carbs: 2.6g

SUMMER SQUASH SOUP

Preparation time: 5 minutes   Cooking time: 20 minutes   Servings: 6

Ingredients:

4lb. summer squash, peeled and cubed
1 sprig sage
½-inch ginger, minced
¼ teaspoon grated nutmeg

3 cups homemade chicken stock
2 cups heavy cream
½ cup toasted pumpkin seeds, unsalted
Salt and pepper, to taste

Directions:

Heat some oil in the pressure cooker. Set the temperature to low.

Add the sage and cook until fragrant.

Place enough squash cubes to cover the bottom of the pressure cooker.

Let them brown for 10 minutes, stirring occasionally.

Add the remaining squash, ginger, nutmeg and chicken stock.

Lock the lid and bring the pressure to high. Maintain the pressure for 15 minutes.

When time is up, use a quick pressure release method.

Discard the sage, add the heavy cream and puree using an immersion blender. Season to taste.

Divide soup between serving bowls and sprinkle with pumpkin seeds before serving.

Nutritional Info: Per serving

Calories: 277   Cholesterol: 55mg   Protein: 9.1g
Total fat: 21.6g   Total Carbs: 13.4g

CHICKEN SPINACH STEW

Preparation time: 5 minutes   Cooking time: 40 minutes   Servings: 4

Ingredients:

4 chicken breasts, skinless and boneless
1 cup baby spinach, roughly chopped
1 cup coconut milk
2 tablespoons ghee

2 tablespoons mild curry powder
4 cups water
1 cup chopped green beans
Fresh ground salt and pepper

Directions:

First cook the chicken: cut chicken breasts in half and place in pressure cooker. Add one cup of water and season with salt and pepper.

Cover with lid tightly and cook on high for 12 minutes.

Once the chicken breasts are done, release the pressure according to manufacturer's Directions.

Remove the chicken and set to plate to cool down. Discard cooking water and place cooking pot back in the electric pressure.

Start the electric pressure and set to medium heat: add ghee and when melted add curry powder. Mix to combine and turn off the electric pressure cooker.

Add coconut milk, beans and remaining water. Stir gently and shut the lid: program the pressure cooker to cook for 30 minutes.

Meanwhile shred the cooked chicken. When the cooking is finished, use a quick pressure release method, remove the lid and stir in baby spinach and cooked chicken. Stir well to combine and additionally season with salt and pepper.

Nutritional Info: Per serving

Calories: 343   Cholesterol: 82mg   Protein: 27.1g
Total fat: 23.8g   Total Carbs: 7.4g

BEEF ZUCCHINI STEW

Preparation time: 5 minutes   Cooking time: 40 minutes   Servings: 6

Ingredients:

2 lb. stewing beef, boneless, cut into 1-inch cubes
1/3 cup ghee
2 tomatoes, pureed
2 cups beef stock, homemade
2-3 fresh thyme springs
1 teaspoon turmeric powder

1 teaspoon ground cumin
½ teaspoon chili powder
½ teaspoon ground ginger
2 celery stalks, cut into ½-inch pieces
2 garlic cloves, crushed
4 zucchinis, trimmed and cubed
Fresh ground salt and pepper – to taste

Directions:

Toss the beef with salt and pepper in a large bowl. Coat evenly and transfer in heated electric pressure with melted ghee. Cook the beef until browned at the medium heat.

If your pressure cooker is small, you can work in batches; transfer bee in a bowl.

Add some of the stock to the electric pressure and bring to simmer; deglaze the cooker by scraping down the brown bits.

Return the beef into pressure cooker and add the spices, onion, carrots, celery, garlic and zucchinis.

Cover and secure the lid. Bring to high pressure. Maintain the pressure for 20 minutes.

Use a natural pressure release. It should take around 10 minutes.

Serve while still hot.

Nutritional Info: Per serving

Calories: 421	Cholesterol: 164mg	Protein: 39.0g
Total fat: 21.4g	Total Carbs: 7.1g	

DUCK AND CHEESE

Preparation time: 5 minutes	Cooking time: 30 minutes	Servings: 4

Ingredients:

1lb. duck leg, boneless
½ cup cream cheese
1 teaspoon dried basil

1 cup heavy cream
1 teaspoon black peppercorns
Salt and pepper, to taste

Directions:

Heat pressure cooker to medium.

Place all the ingredients into a pressure cooker, except the cheese.

Bring the pressure to high and maintain the pressure for 20 minutes.

Use a quick pressure release method to open the lid.

Add the cream cheese and cook for 5 minutes more.

Serve after.

Nutritional Info: Per serving

Calories: 434	Cholesterol: 174mg	Protein: 26.5g
Total fat: 33.9g	Total Carbs: 2.0g	

SALMON CURRY

Preparation time: 5 minutes	Cooking time: 20 minutes	Servings: 6

Ingredients:

4lb. salmon fillets
2 teaspoons lemon juice
1 green bell pepper, seeded, chopped
1 teaspoon hot sauce
1 teaspoons ginger powder
2 garlic cloves
½ fish stock
¼ cup tomato sauce, no sugar added

½ cup coconut milk
4 teaspoons curry powder
1 tablespoon ghee
Salt and pepper, to taste

Directions:

Melt the ghee in a pressure cooker. Set the heat to medium.

Add the garlic and cook until fragrant.

In a bowl, combine the hot sauce, ginger, fish stock, tomato sauce, and curry powder.

Place the salmon in the bottom of slow cooker and cover with bell pepper. Pour over prepared mix and lock the lid. Bring the pressure to high and cook for 15 minutes.

Use a quick pressure release method and open the lid. Stir in the coconut milk and cook for 5 minutes. Serve while still hot.

Nutritional Info: Per serving

Calories: 721   Cholesterol: 208mg   Protein: 49.6
Total fat: 38.8g   Total Carbs: 6.8g

TURKEY, GARLIC AND BUTTER

Preparation time: 5 minutes   Cooking time: 25 minutes   Servings: 4

Ingredients:

1lb. turkey tights, cut into pieces   1 cup chicken broth
4 tablespoons butter   ½ cup coconut aminos
4 garlic cloves, minced   Salt and pepper, to taste

Directions:

Melt the butter in a pressure cooker.

Brown the turkey meat and remove from the cooker.

Add the garlic and cook until fragrant.

Place the turkey back in the cooker and add remaining ingredients.

Lock the lid and bring pressure to high.

Once the pressure starts to rock reduce heat and cook for 25 minutes.

Use a quick pressure release method.

Serve while still hot.

Nutritional Info: Per serving

Calories: 309   Cholesterol: 116mg   Protein: 24.7g
Total fat: 17.5g   Total Carbs: 1.2g

CAULIFLOWER RICE AND CHICKEN SOUP

Preparation time: 5 minutes   Cooking time: 10 minutes   Servings: 4

Ingredients:

6 cups chicken stock   1 cup cauliflower rice (just process
1 large bone-in chicken breast, skin and fat cauliflower florets until you have 1 cup)
trimmed   Fresh ground salt and pepper
2 tablespoon olive oil   Some chopped parsley to garnish
2 ribs celery, diced

Directions:

Set pressure cooker to medium-high heat and heat up the oil.

Add celery and cook for 4-5 minutes or until softened.

Add the garlic and cook for 1 minute. Add cauliflower and stock; stir to combine.

Cut the chicken breast in half and place in pressure cooker; season with salt and pepper.

Lock the lid and bring to high pressure; turn the heat to low, just low enough to maintain the pressure.

Cook for 9 minutes at high pressure and turn off heat; allow pot to stand for 15 minutes.

After 15 minutes place the pressure cooker in the sink and run cold water over the top.

When the pressure is released remove the lid and remove the chicken meat.

When the meat is cool enough to handle shred it finely and return to the pot.

Season additionally with salt and pepper and serve in bowls garnished with salt and pepper.

Nutritional Info: Per serving

Calories: 194	Cholesterol: 58mg	Protein: 20.3g
Total fat: 11.1g	Total Carbs: 2.4g	

PORK AND CHICKEN MIX

Preparation time: 5 minutes	Cooking time: 50 minutes	Servings: 6

Ingredients:

2lb. chicken tights, skinless and boneless
2lb. ground pork
2 tablespoons tomato sauce, low-sugar
1 tablespoon Worcestershire sauce
¼ cup water

1 green bell pepper, seeded, sliced
½ cup shredded cabbage
¼ cup cream cheese
¼ teaspoon smoked paprika
Salt and pepper, to taste

Directions:

Heat non-stick skillet over medium-high heat.

Add the pork and cook until browned. Remove from the heat.

Transfer the pork into a pressure cooker and combine with tomato puree, water, paprika and Worcestershire sauce.

Set the pressure cooker to meat setting and cook for 30 minutes. Use a quick pressure release method and open the lid.

Add the chicken meat, cabbage, cream cheese and bell pepper.

Set the poultry option and cook for 25 minutes.

Use a quick pressure release method and open a lid. Serve while still hot.

Nutritional Info: Per serving

Calories: 490	Cholesterol: 237mg	Protein: 64.5g
Total fat: 13.3g	Total Carbs: 2.9g	

BEEF SOUP WITH SAUERKRAUT

Preparation time: 5 minutes   Cooking time: 15 minutes   Servings: 6

Ingredients:

1lb. minced beef
2oz. bacon
2 tablespoons ghee
2 cups beef stock, homemade
28oz. homemade beef broth
14oz. sauerkraut

1 tablespoon Erythritol
1 tablespoon coconut aminos
1 teaspoon dried chopped sage
2 garlic cloves, minced
1 cup water
Salt and pepper, to taste

Directions:

Heat ghee in the pressure cooker over medium.
Add the bacon and cook until crumbly. Add the beef and cook until browned.
Add drained sauerkraut and stir. Add the remaining ingredients and lock the lid.
Bring the pressure to high and maintain the pressure for 15 minutes.
Once the time is up, release the pressure naturally.
Serve while still hot.

Nutritional Info: Per serving

Calories: 270   Cholesterol: 89mg   Protein: 30.7g
Total fat: 13.9g   Total Carbs: 3.9g

BROCCOLI SOUP

Preparation time: 5 minutes   Cooking time: 10 minutes   Servings: 4

Ingredients:

½ cup butter unsalted
1 ½ lb. broccoli florets
2 cups homemade chicken stock
1 cup heavy cream

1 tablespoons fresh minced ginger
1 teaspoon fresh chopped tarragon
¼ teaspoon caraway seeds, chopped

Directions:

In a pressure cooker combine the butter, ginger, and broccoli.
Season to taste and lock the lid. Bring to high pressure. Maintain the pressure for 10 minutes.
Use a natural pressure release to open the pressure cooker.
Stir in the chicken stock and deglaze any caramelized bits.
Return the cooker to medium heat, uncovered. Stir in the heavy cream.
Reheat the ingredients and puree using immersion blender.
Serve while still hot. Garnish with the tarragon and caraway seeds

Nutritional Info: Per serving

Calories: 384   Cholesterol: 102mg   Protein: 9.0g
Total fat: 35.4g   Total Carbs: 12.6g

SAUERKRAUT SPARE RIBS

Preparation time: 5 minutes   Cooking time: 20 minutes   Servings: 4

Ingredients:

2lb. spare ribs, cut into serving size pieces
1 quart sauerkraut
1 tablespoon olive oil

1 tablespoons Erythritol
1 ½ cups bone broth
Salt and pepper, to taste

Directions:

Heat oil in the pressure cooker.

Add ribs and brown on all sides.

Season with salt and pepper and sprinkle with Erythritol.

Arrange the sauerkraut onto ribs and add the broth.

Lock the lid and bring the pressure to high.

Cook for 15 minutes. Use a quick pressure release method.

Serve while still hot.

Nutritional Info: Per serving

Calories: 676   Cholesterol: 234mg   Protein: 51.4
Total fat: 43.9g   Total Carbs: 6.1g

SPICY PORK LOIN

Preparation time: 5 minutes   Cooking time: 50 minutes   Servings: 4

Ingredients:

1 ½ lb. pork loin
1 tablespoon red wine vinegar
¼ cup olive oil
2 tablespoons lemon juice
1 ½ teaspoons smoked paprika
1 tablespoon ground coriander

1 ½ teaspoons ground cumin
1 tablespoon dried oregano
¼ teaspoon cayenne pepper
2 garlic cloves, minced
1 teaspoon lemon zest

Directions:

Combine the garlic, lemon zest, spices and herbs in a bowl.

Pour the olive oil in a pressure cooker and set the cooker to meat option.

Rum the loin with prepared spice mix and place into a pressure cooker.

Drizzle with vinegar and lemon juice.

Lock the lid and cook for 50 minutes.

Once the time is up, use a quick pressure release method.

Slice before serving. Serve while still hot.

Nutritional Info: Per serving

Calories: 534   Cholesterol: 136mg   Protein: 37.0g
Total fat: 36.8g   Total Carbs: 2.3g

LAMB AND ZUCCHINIS

Preparation time: 5 minutes   Cooking time: 50 minutes   Servings: 4

Ingredients:

16oz. lamb stew meat, cut into pieces
4 zucchinis, trimmed and sliced
14oz. coconut milk
2 garlic cloves, chopped
1 teaspoon coconut oil

1 tablespoon curry powder
1 teaspoon garam masala
½ teaspoon cumin
¼ cup chopped cilantro
Salt and pepper, to taste

Directions:

Heat the coconut oil in a pressure cooker. Add the garlic and cook until fragrant.
Add the lamb meat, zucchinis, coconut milk, and spices.
Bring the pressure to high and maintain for 40 minutes.
Use a quick pressure release method. Open the lid and stir in chopped cilantro.
Serve while still hot.

Nutritional Info: Per serving

Calories: 489   Cholesterol: 102mg   Protein: 26.9g
Total fat: 33.7g   Total Carbs: 13.6g

FAST PORK RIBS

Preparation time: 5 minutes   Cooking time: 15 minutes   Servings: 4

Ingredients:

2lb. pork ribs
1 Cup Low-Carb BBQ sauce
½ cup chicken stock

2 tablespoons bacon fat
Salt and pepper, to taste

Directions:

Cut the ribs into individual portions and season to taste.
Bring the pressure cooker to medium heat. Melt the bacon fat and brown the ribs in the fat. Remove and place aside.
Remove excess oil and pour in the stock to deglaze the cooker.
Place back the ribs into a cooker and pour over ½ cup sauce.
Bing the pressure to high and maintain the pressure for 12 minutes. Use a quick pressure release method.
Toss the ribs with remaining sauce and serve.

Nutritional Info: Per serving

Calories: 690   Cholesterol: 240mg   Protein: 40.6g
Total fat: 46.7g   Total Carbs: 2.9g

Taco Soup

Preparation time: 5 minutes   Cooking time: 20 minutes   Servings: 4

Ingredients:

2 tablespoons olive oil
2 garlic cloves, minced
1 cup chopped celery
2oz. bacon, chopped
2 chicken breasts, skinless and boneless
4 cups homemade chicken stock

3oz. tomato paste, without sugar
1 teaspoon ground cumin
1 teaspoon ground coriander
½ teaspoon smoked paprika
Salt and pepper, to taste

Directions:

Cook bacon in a skillet, until crispy. Place aside and crumble.
In a pressure cooker, combine the olive oil, garlic and celery.
Set the medium heat and cook the vegetables for 3 minutes.
Add the remaining ingredients and lock the lid.
Bring the pressure to high. Maintain the pressure for 10 minutes.
When the time goes off, use a natural pressure release.
Remove the chicken and shred with two forks. Return to the pressure cooker and stir.
Serve with lime wedges and sliced avocado.

Nutritional Info: Per serving

Calories: 209   Cholesterol: 16mg   Protein: 12.7g
Total fat: 15.6g   Total Carbs: 7.1g

Salmon Meatballs with Lemon Sauce

Preparation time: 5 minutes   Cooking time: 20 minutes   Servings: 4

Ingredients:

1lb. ground salmon, wild-caught
2 tablespoons butter
2 garlic cloves, minced
2 tablespoons mustard
1 egg
1 tablespoon almond flour

For the sauce:

2 tablespoon melted ghee
2 garlic cloves, minced
1 lemon, juiced and zested
2 tablespoons mustard
2 cups heavy cream
2 tablespoon chopped chives

Directions:

Melt 1 tablespoon butter in a skillet. Add garlic and cook until fragrant. Remove from the heat.
Combine the garlic with the ground salmon, egg, mustard and almond flour.
Form 20 meatballs from the mixture.
Melt the remaining butter in pressure cooker over medium heat.
Add the meatballs and cook until browned.

Lock the lid and bring pressure to high. Maintain the pressure for 5 minutes. Meanwhile, whisk all the sauce ingredients. Use a quick pressure release method to open the lid. Pour the sauce over salmon meatballs and let it stand for 10 minutes before serving. Serve after.

Nutritional Info: Per serving

Calories: 331

Total fat: 32.3g

Cholesterol: 138mg

Total Carbs: 6.7g

Protein:15.7g

Pesto Pepperoni Lasagna

Preparation time: 5 minutes | Cooking time: 15 minutes | Servings: 4

Ingredients:

15oz. ricotta cheese
1 egg
¼ cup pesto sauce
1 pinch red pepper flakes

4 cups shredded Provolone cheese
2 zucchinis, sliced thinly
6oz. sliced pepperoni
15oz. pizza sauce, no sugar added

Directions:

Combine ricotta, pesto sauce, and 1 cup shredded cheese. Mix well, season to taste and stir in the egg.
Place the zucchinis at the bottom of pressure cooker. Top with pepperoni slices. These will be your lasagna sheets.
Top with ¼ ricotta mixture and ¼ shredded cheese.
Repeat the layers until you have no ingredients left.
Lock the lid and bring the pressure to high. Maintain he pressure for 7 minutes.
Use a quick pressure release method and open the lid.
Place aside to rest for 10 minutes and slice. Serve after.

Nutritional Info: Per serving

Calories: 981

Total fat: 70.7g

Cholesterol: 213mg

Total Carbs: 22.1g

Protein: 61.4g

Chicken Chili Lime Meatballs

Preparation time: 5 minutes | Cooking time: 10 minutes | Servings: 4

Ingredients:

1lb. ground chicken
2 tablespoons flaxseeds meal
2 tablespoons almond flour
½ green bell pepper, chopped
2 tablespoons chopped cilantro
½ teaspoon red pepper flakes
½ lime, juiced and zested
2oz. cheddar cheese

2 tablespoons ghee
Salt and pepper, to taste

For the guacamole:

1 avocado
½ lime, juiced
Salt and pepper, to taste

Directions:

In a bowl, combine the meatballs ingredients, chicken through the cheddar cheese. Season with salt and pepper.

Mix with clean hands and form meatballs from the mixture.

Melt ghee in a pressure cooker and add the meatballs. Cook until browned.

Lock the lid and bring the pressure to high. Maintain the pressure for 5 minutes.

Meanwhile, mash the avocado in a bowl. Stir in the lime juice and season the taste.

Use a quick pressure release method and open the lid.

Serve meatballs with prepared guacamole.

Nutritional Info: Per serving

Calories: 477

Cholesterol: 132mg

Protein: 29.0g

Total fat: 32.9g

Total Carbs: 7.2g

CABBAGE PORK SOUP

Preparation time: 5 minutes

Cooking time: 30 minutes

Servings: 4

Ingredients:

4 tablespoon ghee
1lb. ground pork
4 cups chicken broth, homemade
½ head Savoy cabbage, shredded
1 teaspoon minced garlic

1 teaspoon onion powder
1 teaspoon ground ginger
2/3 cup coconut aminos
Salt, to taste

Directions:

Melt the ghee in a pressure cooker. Add the pork and cook until brown.

Add the remaining ingredients and give it a good stir.

Bring the pressure to high and maintain he pressure for 25 minutes.

Use a quick pressure release to open the lid.

Serve while still hot.

Nutritional Info: Per serving

Calories: 340

Cholesterol: 116mg

Protein: 25.9g

Total fat: 18.2g

Total Carbs: 7.1g

WALNUT CRUSTED SALMON

Preparation time: 5 minutes

Cooking time: 10 minutes

Servings: 2

Ingredients:

1 cup walnuts
¼ teaspoon dried dill
½ tablespoon mustard
8oz. salmon fillets
1 tablespoon olive oil

Salt and pepper, to taste

Directions:

In a food blender, pulse the walnuts, dill, ½ tablespoon olive oil, and mustard.

Pulse until you have a smooth paste.

Brush the salmon with prepared mix.

Coat the pressure cooker with remaining olive oil. Place the salmon into a pressure cooker and lock the lid.

Bring the pressure to high and maintain the pressure for 6 minutes.

Use a natural pressure release method. Open the lid and remove salmon fillets.

Serve while still hot with preferred side dish.

Nutritional Info: Per serving

Calories: 610	Cholesterol: 50mg	Protein: 37.8g
Total fat: 51.7g	Total Carbs: 7.2g	

Beef Burger Casserole

Preparation time: 5 minutes	Cooking time: 20 minutes	Servings: 4

Ingredients:

1lb. ground beef	2 tablespoons no-sugar tomato paste
3 slices bacon	1 tablespoon mustard
½ cup almond flour	2 tablespoons mayonnaise
3 cups chopped cauliflower, riced in a food blender	3 eggs
	4oz. grated Cheddar cheese, divided
1 garlic clove, minced	Salt, to taste

Directions:

Process bacon in a food blender until crumbly and kind of paste.

Combine the bacon with beef, garlic, and place in the heated non-stick skillet.

Cook until browned.

Stir in the cauliflower rice and 2oz. grated cheese. Add the remaining ingredients and stir well.

Line the pressure cooker with parchment paper and transfer in the beef mix. sprinkle with cheese and lock the lid.

Bring the pressure to high and maintain the pressure for 12 minutes.

Use a quick pressure release and open the lid.

Let the casserole rest for 10 minutes. Remove using parchment paper and slice before serving.

Nutritional Info: Per serving

Calories: 434	Cholesterol: 226mg	Protein: 37.3g
Total fat: 23.1g	Total Carbs: 7,6g	

Flavored Balsamic pork

Preparation time: 5 minutes	Cooking time: 30 minutes	Servings: 4

Ingredients:

2lb. pork shoulder	2 tablespoons balsamic vinegar

2 tablespoons Worcestershire sauce
1 garlic clove, minced
1 tablespoon bacon grease
1 cup ranch dressing

1 tablespoon yellow mustard
½ teaspoon chipotle powder
Salt and pepper, to taste

Directions:

Cut the pork into a bite size pieces. Season to taste with salt and pepper.

Combine the remaining ingredients in a bowl.

Place all the ingredients and the pork in a pressure cooker.

Set the pressure to high. Maintain the pressure for 20 minutes.

Use a quick pressure release and open the lid.

Serve pork while still hot.

Nutritional Info: Per serving

Calories: 693
Total fat: 48.4g

Cholesterol: 204mg
Total Carbs: 5.3g

Protein: 43.9g

CHICKEN POT PIE

Preparation time: 15 minutes   Cooking time: 10 minutes   Servings: 6

Ingredients:

6 chicken tights, skinless and boneless
5 slices bacon, chopped
1 garlic clove, minced
½ teaspoon celery seed
4oz. Cheddar cheese
8oz. cream cheese
6 cups spinach
¼ cup chicken broth
Salt, to taste

For the crust:
3 tablespoons Psyllium husk
1/3 cup almond flour
1 egg
3 tablespoons butter
2oz. cream cheese
2oz. cheddar cheese
Salt, to taste

Directions:

Cut the chicken into cubes and season with salt.

Preheat pressure cooker to medium. Toss in the chicken along with bacon.

Cook until chicken is browned. De-glaze the cooker with chicken broth and stir in the cheddar and cream cheese. Toss in the spinach and stir well.

Meanwhile, create the crust: blend all ingredients and form into circle.

Top the chicken with prepared crust and lock the lid.

Bring the pressure to high and maintain the pressure for 8 minutes.

Use a quick pressure release method. Open the cooker and let the pie stand for 5 minutes.

Serve after.

Nutritional Info: Per serving

Calories: 458
Total fat: 33.9g

Cholesterol: 158mg
Total Carbs: 17.9g

Protein: 25.3g

CREAMY SHRIMPS

Preparation time: 5 minutes   Cooking time: 10 minutes   Servings: 2

Ingredients:

For the sauce:

2 tablespoons butter
1 garlic clove, minced
2 chilies, seeds removed
2 tablespoons curry leaves

1oz. sharp Cheddar cheese, grated
½ cup heavy cream
Salt, to taste

For the shrimps:

12 medium shrimps, peeled and deveined

Directions:

Place the shrimps into a pressure cooker.
Season with salt and pepper. In a bowl, combine the sauce ingredients.
Pour over the shrimps and lock the lid.
Bring the pressure to high and cook for 7 minutes.
Use a quick pressure release and open the lid.
Serve shrimps while still hot.

Nutritional Info: Per serving

Calories: 684   Cholesterol: 305mg   Protein: 44.3g
Total fat: 47.4g   Total Carbs: 9.8g

ORANGE DUCK BREASTS

Preparation time: 5 minutes   Cooking time: 30 minutes   Servings: 2

Ingredients:

6oz. duck breast
2 tablespoons butter, melted
1 tablespoon heavy cream
¼ cup water

½ orange, sliced
¼ teaspoon sage
1 cup spinach
Salt and pepper, to taste

Directions:

Score the duck breasts on top of surface. Season with salt and pepper.
Place the butter, heavy cream, water, oranges and sage into a pressure cooker.
Place the duck on top of oranges and lock the lid.
Bring the pressure to high and turn down the heat.
Maintain the pressure for 25 minutes. Use a natural pressure release method.
Open the lid and serve duck breast while still hot.
Drizzle with cooking liquid.

Nutritional Info: Per serving

Calories: 263   Cholesterol: 41mg   Protein: 18.9g
Total fat: 17.8g   Total Carbs: 6.2g

WHOLE BACON WRAPPED CHICKEN

Preparation time: 5 minutes   Cooking time: 30 minutes   Servings: 6

Ingredients:
3lb. whole chicken
4 sprigs fresh thyme
1 small lime, sliced

10 strips bacon
Salt and pepper, to taste

Directions:
Rinse and pat dry the chicken. Rub it with some salt and pepper. Stuff the chicken with thyme, and lime slices. Wrap the bird with bacon slices and place into a pressure cooker. Lock the lid and bring pressure to high. Maintain the pressure for 25 minutes.
Let the pressure release naturally for 15 minutes and quick pressure release the rest of pressure.
Remove, carve and serve.

Nutritional Info: Per serving
Calories: 602   Cholesterol: 237mg   Protein: 47.7g
Total fat: 30.0g   Total Carbs: 0.5g

MOROCCAN MEATBALLS

Preparation time: 15 minutes   Cooking time: 10 minutes   Servings: 4

Ingredients:
1lb. ground lamb
1 tablespoon chopped cilantro
1 tablespoon chopped mint
2 teaspoons chopped thyme
1 teaspoon minced garlic
1 teaspoon ground cinnamon
1 teaspoon ground cumin
¼ teaspoon oregano
¼ teaspoon curry powder
¼ teaspoon allspice

Salt and pepper, to taste

For the sauce:
2 tablespoons coconut water
½ cup coconut cream
1 ½ teaspoons ground cumin
1 tablespoon chopped mint
1 teaspoon lemon juice
½ teaspoon lemon zest
Salt, to taste

Directions:
In a bowl, combine the meatball ingredients, from the lamb through the allspice. Season to taste and stir to combine. Form meatballs from the prepared mixture and place into pressure cooker.
Lock the lid and bring the pressure to high. Meanwhile, blend all the sauce ingredients into a food blender. Cook for 6 minutes. Use a quick pressure release method. Pour in prepared sauce and close the cooker.
Let it stand for 5 minutes before serving. Serve and enjoy.

Nutritional Info: Per serving
Calories: 292   Cholesterol: 102mg   Protein: 23.0g
Total fat: 15.9g   Total Carbs: 3.8g

BEEF STROGANOFF

Preparation time: 10 minutes   Cooking time: 35 minutes   Servings: 4

Ingredients:

¼ cup almond flour
2lb. beef stew meat
2 tablespoons olive oil
2 garlic cloves, minced
1 cup beef broth

3 cups quartered mushrooms
8oz. sour cream
1 tablespoon mustard
Salt and pepper, to taste

Directions:

Place the cubed meat, flour and salt into a baggie. Shake until beef is coated with flour.
Set the pot to saute and add olive oil. Brown the beef in the pot for 5 minutes. Add the garlic and cook for 3 minutes. Add the broth, lock the lid and choose Stew option. Cook the beef for 35 minutes.
Use a quick pressure release method and open the lid. Stir in remaining ingredients and lock the lid. Simmer for 10 minutes or until mushrooms are tender. Adjust seasonings while still hot. Serve after.

Nutritional Info: Per serving

Calories: 668   Cholesterol: 228mg   Protein: 54.1g
Total fat: 37.7g   Total Carbs: 5.6g

PORK CARNITAS

Preparation time: 10 minutes   Cooking time: 60 minutes   Servings: 6

Ingredients:

2 ½ lb. trimmed pork shoulder
3 garlic cloves, cut into silvers
2 teaspoons cumin
½ teaspoon sazon
½ teaspoon dried oregano
1 cup bone broth

2 chipotle peppers in adobo
2 bay leaves
Salt and pepper, fresh ground
2 avocados, sliced
1 cup sour cream

Directions:

Season pork with fresh ground salt and pepper. Brown pork in a skillet for 5 minutes.
Make 1-inch deep pockets in the pork and place in the garlic silvers.
Season pork with cumin, sazon, oregano, and garlic powder.
Place in the pressure coooker and add the chicken broth, aong with adobo peppers.
Bring the pressure to medium. Cook for 60 minutes.
Use a quick pressure release method and open the lid. Gently pull the pork with two forks.
Serve with avocado and sour cream.

Nutritional Info: Per serving

Calories: 440   Cholesterol: 127mg   Protein: 32.3g
Total fat: 26.6g   Total Carbs: 8.3g

Thai Beef Curry

Preparation time: 5 minutes   Cooking time: 30 minutes   Servings: 4

Ingredients:

1 ½ lb. beef brisket, cubed
1 teaspoon salt
½ tablespoon vegetable oil
1 tablespoon Thai Curry Paste
1 cup coconut milk

1 tablespoon fresh apple juice
1 tablespoons coconut aminos
2 kaffire leaves
½ egg plant, trimmed and cut into chunks
A handful of chopped cilantro

Directions:

Season beef with salt. Season the egg plant with salt and place aside for 20 minutes.

Heat oil in the pressure cooker. Once the oil is hot, add the curry paste and stir until fragrant.

Pour in coconut milk, apple juice, coconut aminos, and kaffire leaves.

Stir well and toss in the beef and eggplant. Bring the pressure to high and cook for 30 minutes.

When the time is up, let the pressure come down naturally.

Open the lid, adjust seasonings. Serve while still hot, garnished with chopped cilantro.

Nutritional Info: Per serving

Calories: 515   Cholesterol: 152mg   Protein: 43.6g
Total fat: 26,8g   Total Carbs: 13.4g

Buttery Salmon Fillets

Preparation time: 10 minutes   Cooking time: 20 minutes   Servings: 4

Ingredients:

4 4oz. thick salmon fillets
1 lemon juiced
2 tablespoons butter
1 tablespoon chili pepper

1 sprig thyme
Salt and pepper, to taste
1 cup water

Directions:

Season the salmon with lemon juice, chili pepper, salt and pepper.

Insert the steam rack or basket into the instant pot.

Place the salmon fillets onto piece of parchment paper, one fillet per one piece.

Top each fillet 1with ½ tablespoon butter. Add thyme.

Place the salmon fillets onto rack and pour water into the pot.

Lock the lid and bring the pressure to high. Cook for 5 minutes.

Once the time is off, use a quick pressure release.

Open the Pressure cooker and remove salmon. Serve immediately.

Nutritional Info: Per serving

Calories: 203   Cholesterol: 65mg   Protein: 15.1g
Total fat: 12.8g   Total Carbs: 0,4g

DUCK AND VEGETABLES

Preparation time: 5 minutes   Cooking time: 25 minutes   Servings: 4

Ingredients:

2lb. duck tights, skinless and boneless
1 cup broccoli florets
1 cup green beans
2 cups chicken stock

1-inch ginger, minced
2 garlic cloves, chopped
1 teaspoon salt

Directions:

Cut the duck meat into a bite size pieces.
Place the duck and the remaining ingredients into the pressure cooker.
Set the pressure to high. Maintain the pressure for 25 minutes.
Use the quick pressure release method and unlock the lid.
Serve while still hot.

Nutritional Info: Per serving

Calories: 479   Cholesterol: 202mg   Protein: 44.8g
Total fat: 25.8g   Total Carbs: 4.3g

CHUCK ROAST

Preparation time: 15 minutes   Cooking time: 60 minutes   Servings: 6

Ingredients:

3lb. chuck roast
3 tablespoons olive oil
2 tablespoons mustard
2 teaspoons paprika

2 tablespoons sesame seeds flour
2 tablespoons ranch dressing
2 cups beef broth
Salt and pepper, to taste

Directions:

Heat olive oil in the pressure cooker.
Brown the chuck roast on all sides. Remove from the cooker.
Add small amount of broth to deglaze the cooker.
Add the ranch dressing and sesame seeds flour. Cook for 2 minutes.
Place the meat back in the cooker along with remaining ingredients.
Lock the lid and bring the pressure to high.
Cook for 1 hour. Use a quick pressure release method.
Open the lid and serve after.

Nutritional Info: Per serving

Calories: 584   Cholesterol: 229mg   Protein: 47.6g
Total fat: 27.5g   Total Carbs: 2.3g

*F*ENNEL *P*OACHED *S*ALMON

Preparation time: 5 minutes   Cooking time: 10 minutes   Servings: 4

Ingredients:

16oz. salmon fillets, skin on
1 lemon, zested
1 teaspoon fennel seeds
4 black peppercorns

1 teaspoon white wine vinegar
2 ½ cups chicken stock
¼ cup chopped fresh dill
Salt and pepper, to taste

Directions:

Season the salmon fillets with salt and pepper. Place onto trivet.

Insert the rivet into pressure cooker.

Pour the stock and vinegar over fish and top with the herbs and zest.

Lock the lid and bring the pressure to high. Maintain the pressure for 5 minutes.

Use a quick pressure release method. Open the lid and serve fish immediately.

Nutritional Info: Per serving

Calories: 166   Cholesterol: 50mg   Protein: 22.1g
Total fat: 8.5g   Total Carbs: 2.5g

*S*HREDDED *B*EEF

Preparation time: 15 minutes   Cooking time: 50 minutes   Servings: 6

Ingredients:

2 ½ lb. beef roast, cut into 1-inch cubes
2 garlic cloves, minced
½ cup chili sauce

½ cup water
2 tablespoons olive oil
2 cups ranch dressing

Directions:

Heat the oil in a pressure cooker.

Add garlic and cook until fragrant.

Add the meat and cook until browned.

Add water and chili sauce. Lock the lid and bring the pressure to high.

Maintain the pressure for 50 minutes. Use a quick pressure release and open the lid.

Shred the beef and place back in the cooker. Stir in the ranch dressing and let it rest for 10 minutes.
Serve after.

Nutritional Info: Per serving

Calories: 419   Cholesterol: 169mg   Protein: 38.5g
Total fat: 16.8g   Total Carbs: 5.0g

QUAIL, MUSHROOMS, AND CHEESE

Preparation time: 10 minutes   Cooking time: 20 minutes   Servings: 2

Ingredients:

4oz. quail drums
2 tablespoons butter
16 Portobello mushrooms, sliced

1 ½ cups sharp Cheddar cheese
Salt and pepper, to taste

Directions:

Melt the butter in a pressure cooker.
Add quail drums and brown slightly. Remove the quail and cook the mushrooms for 3-4 minutes.
Place the quail drums into the cooker and add the remaining ingredients.
Lock the lid and bring the pressure to high.
Maintain the pressure for 15 minutes.
Use a natural pressure release method. Open the lid, adjust seasonings and serve.

Nutritional Info: Per serving

Calories: 595   Cholesterol: 120mg   Protein: 44.2g
Total fat: 44.0g   Total Carbs: 5.9g

MEAT BLEND

Preparation time: 5 minutes   Cooking time: 50 minutes   Servings: 8

Ingredients:

½ lb. ground lamb
½ lb. ground pork
½ lb. ground beef
½ lb. ground chicken
4 eggs, whisked
4 tablespoons butter

2 cups chicken broth
2 cups heavy cream
2 teaspoons minced ginger
2 garlic cloves, minced
1 green bell pepper, chopped
Salt and pepper, to taste

Directions:

Melt the butter in a pressure cooker. Add the garlic and ginger. Cook until fragrant.
Combine all the ingredients in a large bowl.
Transfer in a pressure cooker.
Lock the lid and bring the pressure to high.
Maintain the pressure for 50 minutes. Use a natural pressure release and open the lid.
Serve while still hot.

Nutritional Info: Per serving

Calories: 403   Cholesterol: 235mg   Protein: 27.1g
Total fat: 26.4g   Total Carbs: 2.9g

PORK AND BRUSSELS SPROUTS

Preparation time: 15 minutes   Cooking time: 40 minutes   Servings: 4

Ingredients:

1 ½ lb. ground pork
1lb. Brussels Sprouts, quartered
2 tablespoons olive oil
2 cups heavy cream

1 teaspoon ground coriander
1 teaspoon ground cumin
2oz. cheddar cheese
Salt and pepper, to taste

Directions:

Heat olive oil in a pressure cooker.

Add the spices and cook until fragrant. Toss in the pork and cook until browned.

Add heavy cream and lock the lid. Bring the pressure to high.

Maintain the pressure for 30 minutes. Use a quick pressure release method. Open the lid and toss in the Brussels sprouts.

Lock the lid and high-pressure for 3 minutes.

Use a quick pressure release and open the lid. Serve while still hot.

Nutritional Info: Per serving

Calories: 618   Cholesterol: 221mg   Protein: 43.2g
Total fat: 40.4g   Total Carbs: 12.4g

PRESSURE COOKER MEATLOAF

Preparation time: 5 minutes   Cooking time: 30 minutes   Servings: 6

Ingredients:

3lb. ground beef
1 ¼ cups shredded pork rinds
4 eggs, whisked
10oz. cooked mushrooms (in a pan)

¾ cup grated Parmesan cheese
2 garlic cloves, minced
3 teaspoons dried basil
Salt and pepper, to taste

Directions:

In a mixing bowl, combine all the ingredients.

Form a meatloaf from the mixture with the help of aluminum foil.

Place the trivet in a pressure cooker.

Pour in 2 cups water and insert the trivet.

Lock the lid and set the pressure to high.

Maintain the pressure for 20 minutes.

Use a quick pressure release method.

Open the lid and serve meatloaf.

Nutritional Info: Per serving

Calories: 371   Cholesterol: 209mg   Protein: 44.1g
Total fat: 15.7g   Total Carbs: 1.3g

SWEET AND SOUR CHICKEN

Preparation time: 5 minutes   Cooking time: 20 minutes   Servings: 2

Ingredients:

8oz. chicken breasts, boneless
2 tablespoons olive oil
½ teaspoon liquid stevia
¼ cup white wine vinegar

½ tablespoon coconut aminos
½ teaspoon minced garlic
½ teaspoon minced ginger

Directions:

Heat olive oil in a pressure cooker.
Add garlic and ginger and cook until fragrant.
Toss in the remaining ingredients and lock the lid.
Bring the pressure to high. Maintain the pressure for 10 minutes.
Use a quick pressure release. Open the lid and serve chicken.

Nutritional Info: Per serving

Calories: 300   Cholesterol: 87mg   Protein: 22.9g
Total fat: 17.5g   Total Carbs: 0.8g

Ice creams...as desserts

CHOCOLATE ICE CREAM

Preparation time: 5 minutes
Servings: 4

Ingredients:

16 oz. of heavy cream
4 oz. cocoa powder
4 oz. of unsweetened cashew, coconut or almond milk
4 oz. of powdered Erythritol

4 large organic or free range egg yolks
3 oz. of chopped chocolate
1/2 teaspoon of vanilla extract
1/2 teaspoon of Stevia

Directions:

Pour cream, half the cacao powder, cashew milk and sweetener into a medium sized saucepan, and place on the cooker at medium heat. Whisk thoroughly until the mixture is completely combined.
Whisk egg yolks and add the hot cream mixture. Whisk continuously for a thick consistency.
Add the chopped chocolate, and let it sit until melted and then whisk until the mixture is smooth
Transfer the cream mix into a bowl and set it on top of an ice bath for 15 minutes, or the temperature has cooled down completely. Tightly wrap the mixture up in plastic, and set it in the freezer for 3 hours.
Add the other half of the cashew milk, as well as the vanilla extract and Stevia .
If using an ice-cream maker: Pour the contents into the ice-cream maker, and follow the directions as per the manufacturer. Without an ice-cream maker: Transfer the mixture into a freezable container and set it in the freezer. Blend the mixture every hour to eliminate ice crystals, and continue to freeze until the ice- cream has completely frozen.

Nutritional Info: Per serving

Calories: 626
Total fat: 59.5g

Cholesterol: 270mg
Total Carbs: 16.0g

Protein: 8.3g

PEACHY LAVENDER ICE CREAM

Preparation Time: 15 minutes + inactive time

Servings: 8

Ingredients:

2 14oz. cans heavy cream
1 cup raspberries

½ teaspoon liquid stevia
¼ teaspoon dried lavender flowers

Directions:

Puree the raspberries and lavender in a food blender.
Add the heavy cream and Stevia. Process until smooth.
Transfer the mixture into ice cream making machine and process according to manufacturer's directions.

Serve after as a soft ice cream.

If you want firm ice cream, pop in the freezer for 4 hours.

Note: if you do not own the ice cream making a machine, transfer the mixture into a plastic container and freeze overnight.

Nutritional Info: Per serving

Calories: 350

Cholesterol: 136mg

Protein: 2.6g

Total fat: 36.8g

Total Carbs: 4.6g

Tarragon Peach Ice cream

Preparation Time: 20 minutes + inactive time   Servings: 8

Ingredients:

1 ½ cups chopped peaches

2 14oz. cans heavy cream

1 bunch tarragon

1 tablespoon arrowroot powder

½ teaspoon liquid Stevia

Directions:

Bruise the tarragon in a mortar and pestle.

Place the tarragon in a saucepot with heavy cream. Bring to a simmer, but do not boil.

Remove from the heat and place aside to cool completely.

Puree the peaches with stevia in a food blender. Pulse until smooth.

Discard the tarragon and pour the infused milk into the blender. Pulse with peaches until blended.

Churn the ice cream in the ice cream machine maker according to the manufacturer's directions.

Serve after. Note: if you do not own the ice cream making a machine, transfer the mixture into a plastic container and freeze overnight.

Nutritional Info: Per serving

Calories: 353

Cholesterol: 136mg

Protein: 2.7g

Total fat: 36.8g

Total Carbs: 5.4g

Rosemary Ice Cream

Preparation Time: 40 minutes + inactive time   Servings: 6

Ingredients:

2 cups heavy cream

1 cup coconut milk

1 teaspoon liquid stevia

½ teaspoon vanilla paste

1 large rosemary sprig

1 pinch salt

Directions:

Combine heavy cream, coconut milk, stevia, and rosemary in a saucepan. Stir over medium heat and bring just to boil. Remove from the heat and cover. Let the mixture steep for 30 minutes.

Discard the rosemary sprig and stir in the coconut cream.

Transfer mixture to ice cream maker and follow manufacturer's directions.

At this point, you can either serve soft ice cream of freeze for 4 hours. With this step, you will have firm ice cream.

Note: if you do not own the ice cream making a machine, transfer the mixture into a plastic container and freeze overnight.

Nutritional Info: Per serving

Calories: 230   Cholesterol: 55mg   Protein: 1.9g
Total fat: 24.3g   Total Carbs: 3.3g

COFFEE CINNAMON ICE CREAM

Preparation Time: 10 minutes + inactive time   Servings: 12

Ingredients:

1 cup fresh brewed coffee
1 tablespoon finely ground coffee
1 ½ cups cashews, soaked in water for 4 hours
1 cup heavy cream

½ teaspoon stevia
1 teaspoon cinnamon
1 pinch salt
½ teaspoon ground cardamom
2 tablespoons melted coconut oil

Directions:

Drain and rinse the cashews.
Place the cashews with almond milk in a food blender. Pulse until smooth.
Add the brewed coffee, stevia, cinnamon, salt, cardamom, and coconut oil.
Blend together until combined. Stir in the ground coffee.
Transfer mixture to ice cream maker and follow manufacturer's directions.
Transfer the ice cream to a freezer-friendly container and allow to freeze until firm.
Scoop and serve after.
Note: if you do not own the ice cream making a machine, transfer the mixture into a plastic container and freeze overnight.

Nutritional Info: Per serving

Calories: 153   Cholesterol: 14mg   Protein: 3.9g
Total fat: 14.9g   Total Carbs: 5.1g

EASY CHAI ICE CREAM

Preparation Time: 15 minutes + inactive time   Servings: 6

Ingredients:

1 black tea bag
1 ¼ cups heavy cream
3 cardamom pods, crushed
4 cloves
1 cinnamon stick
1 pinch nutmeg

2 black peppercorns
1 teaspoon stevia
¼ teaspoon ginger, fresh and grated
¼ teaspoon allspice
¼ teaspoon vanilla paste
1 cup light whipping cream

Directions:

Bring all ingredients, except light whipping cream and tea bag to a gentle simmer in a saucepot.

Add tea bag and steep for 5 minutes. Pour mixture through strainer and place aside to cool.

Combine prepared chai with almond milk and refrigerate for 1 hour.

Transfer into ice cream machine and process according to manufacturer's directions.

Serve as soft ice cream.

Nutritional Info: Per serving

Calories: 145	Cholesterol: 56mg	Protein: 0.9g
Total fat: 15.5g	Total Carbs: 1.5g	

VANILLA ICE CREAM

Preparation Time: 15 minutes + inactive time   Servings: 8

Ingredients:

15oz. heavy cream
15oz. light cream
1 tablespoon vanilla paste
1 ½ teaspoon stevia

1 vanilla bean, seeds scraped out
4 teaspoon arrowroot powder
1 tablespoon water

Directions:

In a medium pot, whisk the coconut milk, vanilla paste, and vanilla seeds. Bring to a simmer over medium-high heat. Cover the pot and simmer for 5 minutes. Remove from the heat and stir in stevia.

Whisk the arrowroot powder with water and slowly drizzle into the coconut milk. Place the mixture over heat and remove as soon as it simmers. Pour into a metal container and refrigerate for 2 hours.

Churn the ice cream in a machine according to the manufacturer's directions. Serve after.

Note: if you do not own the ice cream making a machine, transfer the mixture into a freezer-friendly plastic container and freeze overnight.

Nutritional Info: Per serving

Calories: 339	Cholesterol: 132mg	Protein: 2.2g
Total fat: 36.1g	Total Carbs: 3.0g	

STRAWBERRY ICE CREAM

Preparation Time: 10 minutes + inactive time   Servings: 8

Ingredients:

1lb. fresh strawberries
¼ teaspoon liquid stevia

2 cups heavy cream
2 teaspoons lemon juice

Directions:

Combine all ingredients in a food blender.

Mix until just smooth. Transfer the mixture into the freezer-friendly container. Freeze for 30 minutes.

Churn the ice cream in the machine according to the manufacturer's directions.

Serve immediately.

Note: if you do not own the ice cream making a machine, transfer the mixture into a plastic container and freeze overnight.

Nutritional Info: Per serving

Calories: 122

Cholesterol: 41mg

Protein: 1.2g

Total fat: 12.3g

Total Carbs: 4.2g

Mexican Coffee Ice Cream

Preparation Time: 15 minutes + inactive time

Servings: 4

Ingredients:

1 cup heavy cream

1 ½ cups ice

½ teaspoon cinnamon, like Ceylon cinnamon

¼ teaspoon almond extract

¼ teaspoon liquid stevia

½ cup strong brewed coffee, fresh

Directions:

Bring milk to a simmer in a saucepot over medium heat; add maple syrup. Place aside to cool.

Pour the milk into a food blender and add remaining ingredients; pulse to blend thoroughly.

Pour into plastic container and chill for 1 hour.

Transfer the mixture into ice cream machine and process according to manufacturer's directions.

Scoop and serve.

Nutritional Info: Per serving

Calories: 105

Cholesterol: 41mg

Protein: 1.6g

Total fat: 11.1g

Total Carbs: 1.1g

Espresso Ice Cream

Preparation Time: 5 minutes + inactive time

Servings: 6

Ingredients:

2 shots espresso

1 ½ cups coconut milk

¾ teaspoon stevia

1 teaspoon vanilla paste

Directions:

In a blender, combine all the ingredients.

Pulse until combined.

Chill the mixture for 2 hours.

Transfer mixture to ice cream maker and follow manufacturer's directions.

At this point, you can either serve soft ice cream of freeze for 4 hours. With this step, you will have firm ice cream.

Note: if you do not own the ice cream making a machine, transfer the mixture into a plastic container and freeze overnight.

Nutritional Info: Per serving

Calories: 138
Total fat: 14,5g

Cholesterol: 0mg
Total Carbs: 3.3g

Protein: 1.4g

SWIRLY ICE CREAM

Preparation Time: 10 minutes + inactive time

Servings: 6

Ingredients:

14oz. heavy cream
½ teaspoon liquid stevia
1 teaspoon lime zest

1 teaspoon lime juice
1 ¼ cups raspberries, fresh
1 ¼ cups peaches, chopped and fresh

Directions:

Combine heavy cream and stevia in a bowl. Divide cream into two equal parts and place one part in a food processor; add in raspberries, lime zest, and juice. Process until smooth and pour into plastic container. Freeze for 30 minutes.

Meanwhile, combine remaining cream with peaches and process until smooth. Pour the mixture over raspberry mix, swirl with a spoon and freeze for 4-6 hours.

Scoop and serve.

Nutritional Info: Per serving

Calories: 254
Total fat: 24.7g

Cholesterol: 91mg
Total Carbs: 6.9g

Protein: 2.8g

BANANA CACAO POPSICLES

Preparation Time: 5 minutes + inactive time

Servings: 6

Ingredients:

1 banana
2 tablespoons cacao powder, raw
2 cups heavy cream

½ teaspoon vanilla, pure
10 drops stevia

Directions:

Combine all ingredients, by order in a food blender.
Pulse until smooth and blended thoroughly.
Pour the mixture into silicone molds, close with cap and store into the freezer for 4-6 hours or until firm.
Serve when ready.

Nutritional Info: Per serving

Calories: 157
Total fat: 15.0g
Cholesterol: 55mg

Total Carbs: 5.7g
Protein: 1.3g

*B*ERRY POPSICLES

Preparation Time: 10 minutes + inactive time   Servings: 10 popsicles

Ingredients:

14oz. Greek yogurt
2 cup heavy cream
1 teaspoon liquid stevia

2 tablespoons lime juice
4oz. blueberries, fresh
4oz. raspberries, fresh

Directions:

Combine berries with half the stevia and lime juice. Mash with for and place aside for 15 minutes.
In separate bowl combine remaining ingredients and when time, stir in berries mix. Transfer mixture into silicone molds and close with cap. Store in freezer until firm and serve after.

Nutritional Info: Per serving

Calories: 125   Cholesterol: 35mg   Protein: 4.8g
Total fat: 9.8g   Total Carbs: 5.3g

*C*ACAO FUDGE SICKLES

Preparation Time: 10 minutes + inactive time   Servings: 6

Ingredients:

2 cups heavy cream
1 teaspoon vanilla paste
½ cup cocoa powder

½ teaspoon liquid stevia
½ cup coconut cream

Directions:

Combine all ingredients in a saucepan. Bring to a gentle simmer and whisk until blended.
Place aside to cool. Pour cooled mixture into 6 molds and freeze until solid.
Serve after.

Nutritional Info: Per serving

Calories: 200   Cholesterol: 55mg   Protein: 2.8g
Total fat: 20.5g   Total Carbs: 6.2g

*P*ISTACHIO ICE CREAM

Preparation Time: 10 minutes + inactive time   Servings: 8

Ingredients:

1 ½ cups heavy cream
2 avocados, pitted, peeled
¼ cups cashews, soaked overnight
1 banana
2 teaspoons vanilla paste

½ teaspoon liquid stevia
½ teaspoon almond extract
1 pinch salt
1 cup raw pistachios, shelled

Directions:

Place all ingredients, except the pistachios in a food blender. Process on high until smooth.

Transfer into a freezer-friendly container and sprinkle with pistachios.

Pop in the freezer and chill for 4-5 hours.

Serve after.

Nutritional Info: Per serving

Calories: 259   Cholesterol: 31mg   Protein: 4.7g

Total fat: 24.7g   Total Carbs: 10.7g

WALNUT ICE CREAM

Preparation Time: 10 minutes + inactive time   Servings: 6

Ingredients:

14oz. coconut milk   1 tablespoon arrowroot powder
14oz. heavy cream   1 teaspoon vanilla paste
½ teaspoon liquid stevia   1 cup chopped walnuts

Directions:

Whisk the arrowroot powder with 4 tablespoons coconut milk.

Heat the remaining coconut milk and bring just to a simmer. Remove from the heat and whisk in the arrowroot powder mix and vanilla paste.

Place aside to cool down. Once it reaches room temperature, transfer to an ice cream machine. Churn the ice cream according to manufacturer's direction. In the last minutes, add the chopped walnuts.

Scoop and serve.

Nutritional Info: Per serving

Calories: 509   Cholesterol: 91mg   Protein: 7.9g

Total fat: 52.5g   Total Carbs: 7.6g

KEY LIME ICE CREAM

Preparation Time: 10 minutes + inactive time   Servings: 4

Ingredients:

¾ cup key lime juice
1 cup heavy cream   2 avocados, peeled, pitted
1 teaspoon vanilla paste   Stevia, to taste
½ cup softened coconut oil   1 pinch salt

Directions:

Combine all ingredients in a blender. Blend until completely smooth.

Transfer the mixture into ice cream machine and churn for 30 minutes.

Serve immediately if you prefer soft ice cream. For the firmer version, transfer the mixture to freezer-friendly container and freeze up to 2 hours.

Note: if you do not own the ice cream making a machine, transfer the mixture into a plastic container and freeze overnight.

Nutritional Info: Per serving

Calories: 543   Cholesterol: 41mg   Protein: 3.5g
Total fat: 58.0g   Total Carbs: 9.5g

MINT CHOCOLATE DELICACY

Preparation Time: 10 minutes + inactive time   Servings: 6

Ingredients:

14oz. heavy cream   ½ teaspoon peppermint extract
6oz. light cream   1 tablespoon arrowroot powder
1 cup almond milk   ½ teaspoon liquid stevia
2 tablespoons raw cacao powder

Directions:

In a food blender, combine all the ingredients.
Blend on high until combined.
Churn an ice cream machine according to the manufacturer's directions.
Scoop and serve.
Note: if you do not own the ice cream making a machine, transfer the mixture into plastic container and freeze for 6 hours, stirring each hour.

Nutritional Info: Per serving

Calories: 404   Cholesterol: 122mg   Protein: 3.9g
Total fat: 42.8g   Total Carbs: 5.0g

COCONUT GELATO

Preparation Time: 10 minutes + inactive time   Servings: 8

Ingredients:

5 egg yolks organic or free range   3 tablespoons of Stevia
2 cups of coconut cream   1oz of unsweetened shredded coconut
1 cup of full fat cream   1 tablespoon of vanilla extract

Directions:

Add egg yolks to a bowl, mix and set
Pour the cream, coconut cream, and the sweetener into a saucepan, set onto a stove on a moderate temperature and whisk until the sweetener has disintegrated, and the mixture has started to bubble lightly.
Add the egg yolks to the cream mixture and whisk thoroughly.
Pour in the vanilla extract, and keep stirring until the mixture thickens.
Remove the saucepan from the stove,
and set the mixture aside to cool down.

Transfer the ingredients into a bowel,
and set it in the fridge for 30 60 minutes.
Store in freezer until firm. Scoop and serve after.

Nutritional Info: Per serving

Calories: 228	Cholesterol: 152mg	Protein: 3.4g
Total fat: 22.7g	Total Carbs: 4.3g	

BLUEBERRY ICE CREAM

Preparation Time: 10 minutes + inactive time   Servings: 6

Ingredients:

1.5 cups fresh blueberries
1.5 cup heavy cream
4 whole eggs
1 cup full fat milk

1 cup filtered water
½ cup powdered Eyrthritol
1 teaspoon vanilla paste
1 pinches salt

Directions:

In a saucepan, whisk the water, milk, eggs, sugar, and salt.
Heat the mix over medium-high heat and bring to a gentle bubble.
Strain into a wide bowl and cool.
Whisk in the vanilla, whipping cream and fresh blueberries.
Cover and chill for 2 hours. Pour the mix into an ice cream making machine and process according to manufacturers Directions.
NOTE: If you do not own the ice cream making a machine, cover the ice cream mix and freeze for 4-6 hours, stirring after each hour to prevent ice crystal formation. Serve as usual.

Nutritional Info: Per serving

Calories: 187	Cholesterol: 154mg	Protein:6.9g
Total fat: 15.0g	Total Carbs: 8.3g	

RASPBERRY CHEESECAKE ICE CREAM

Preparation Time: 10 minutes + inactive time   Servings: 10

Ingredients:

1 ½ cup fresh pureed raspberries
1 cup whole milk
1 cup whipping cream

5oz. cream cheese softened
1 cup powdered Eyrthritol
1 teaspoon vanilla paste

Directions:

Strain the pureed raspberries through fine mesh sieve, pressing with a back of the spoon. You are doing this to remove those tiny raspberry seeds.
Cream the sugar and cream cheese in a bowl.
Whisk in the pureed raspberries and milk. Once combined whisk in the whipping cream and vanilla paste.

Pour the mixture into an ice cream machine maker and process according to manufacturer Directions.
NOTE: If you do not own the ice cream making machine cover the ice cream mix and freeze for 4-6 hours, stirring after each hour to prevent ice crystal formation. Serve as usual.

Nutritional Info: Per serving

Calories: 109	Cholesterol: 31mg	Protein: 3.3g
Total fat: 9.6g	Total Carbs: 4.0g	

BANANA COCONUT ICE CREAM

Preparation Time: 10 minutes + inactive time   Servings: 10

Ingredients:

3 ripe mashed bananas
6 egg yolks
1 cup powdered Eyrthritol
15oz. coconut cream

2 teaspoons vanilla paste
2 cups half-and-half
2 cups sweetened coconut flakes

Directions:

Preheat oven to 350F and line baking sheet with parchment paper. Spread the coconut flakes onto a baking sheet and bake for 10 minutes, or until toasted.
In a saucepan, whisk the egg yolks, milk, and Erythritol. Heat over medium heat and bring to a very gentle simmer. Cook, whisking for 20 minutes or until mixture thickens.
Remove from the heat and stir in the coconut flakes, coconut cream, banana, and half-and-half.
Fold in vanilla and stir until combined thoroughly. Pour the mix into a wide bowl, cover and refrigerate for 2 hours.
Pour the mixture into an ice cream making machine and process according to manufacturer directions.
NOTE: If you do not own the ice cream making a machine, cover the ice cream mix and freeze for 4-6 hours, stirring after each hour to prevent ice crystal formation. Serve as usual.

Nutritional Info: Per serving

Calories: 271	Cholesterol: 144mg	Protein: 5.8g
Total fat: 23.8g	Total Carbs: 12.6g	

BUTTERMILK ICE CREAM

Preparation Time: 10 minutes + inactive time   Servings: 8

Ingredients:

1 cup buttermilk
2 cups plums, peeled and chopped
1 cup heavy cream
2 cups half-and-half

6 egg yolks
2 tablespoons lemon juice
Powdered Erythritol, to taste
Small pinch salt

Directions:

In a saucepan whisk the buttermilk, heavy cream, half-and-half, egg yolks and Erythritol.

Cook over medium-high heat, whisking for 12 minutes or until slightly thickened.

Pour the prepared mixture into a large bowl and chill for 2 hours.

While the ice cream is chilling, prepare the plums: stir together the plums, salt and remaining sugar in a saucepan.

Cook over medium heat for 10-12 minutes or until plums are very tender. Remove from heat and allow cooling for 15 minutes. Stir in the lemon juice cover and freeze.

Pour prepared egg yolk mixture into an ice cream maker machine and process according to manufacturer directions. Serve with frozen plums.

NOTE: If you do not own the ice cream making a machine, cover the ice cream mix and freeze for 4-6 hours, stirring after each hour to prevent ice crystal formation. Dollop frozen plum mixture over frozen ice and gently swirl.

Nutritional Info: Per serving

Calories: 191
Total fat: 16.2g
Cholesterol: 202mg
Total Carbs: 7.0g
Protein: 6.3g

Other Desserts...

RAW CHOCOLATE BALLS

Preparation Time: 10 minutes · Servings: 16

Ingredients:

1 cup walnuts
1 cup almonds
¼ cup dates
½ cup almond butter
1 teaspoon vanilla extract

½ teaspoon orange extract
½ cup cocoa powder
¼ teaspoon salt
1 teaspoon cinnamon
½ teaspoon water

Directions:

Place almonds, walnuts and salt in food processor. Pulse until combined; add remaining ingredient and pulse again until you have sticky mixture, well blended. Transfer the mixture in a bowl and form balls with hands. You can roll in coconut shreds or chopped walnuts before serving. Serve with love.

Nutritional Info: Per serving

Calories: 101
Total fat: 9.2g

Cholesterol: 0mg
Total Carbs: 4.8g

Protein: 3.8g

PALEO LAVA CAKE

Preparation Time: 10 minutes · Cooking time: 12 minutes · Servings: 4

Ingredients:

4 oz. cacao powder or sugar-free chocolate
2 eggs
1 teaspoon almond flour
2 teaspoons cocoa powder
Dash of salt

½ teaspoon almond extract
½ teaspoon stevia
4 tablespoons coconut oil
½ teaspoon cardamom

Preparation method:

Preheat oven to 350F and grease ramekins with some coconut oil. Combine coconut oil and chocolate in ovenproof dish. Microwave on high until chocolate is melted. Stir to combine. In a bowl whisk the eggs, stevia salt and almond extract until fluffy. Pour into egg mixture and add cocoa powder and almond flour. Gently combine the ingredients until well combined. Pour batter into prepared ramekins and place them on baking tray. Bake in preheated oven for 10-12 minutes. Set aside to cool and dust with cocoa powder before serving. Serve with love.

Nutritional Info: Per serving

Calories: 269
Total fat: 23.3g

Cholesterol: 82mg
Total Carbs: 9.0g

Protein: 10.5g

KETO COOKIES

Preparation Time: 10 minutes
Cooking time: 7 minutes
Servings: 12

Ingredients:

1 ½ cup almond flour
¼ teaspoon baking soda
Dash of salt
¼ cup melted coconut oil

½ teaspoon liquid Stevia
1 egg
½ teaspoon vanilla extract
½ cup dark chocolate chips, no sugar added

Directions:

Preheat oven to 350F and line baking tray with parchment paper. Combine dry ingredients in a bowl until well mixed. In a separate bowl whisk egg, honey, coconut oil and vanilla extract. Fold wet ingredients in the dry ones and whisk until combined. Stir in the chocolate chips and spoon the batter onto lined baking tray. Slightly flatten the cookies with spatula and bake for 5-7 minutes. Serve when cooled and keep in airtight container. Serve with love.

Nutritional Info: Per serving

Calories: 96
Total fat: 9.2g

Cholesterol: 15mg
Total Carbs: 4.7g

Protein: 2.5g

ALMOND TRUFFLES

Preparation Time: 10 minutes

Servings: 10

Ingredients:

¼ cup sugar-free syrup
½ cup butter
1 teaspoon almond extract
½ teaspoon cherry liqueur
1 ½ tablespoon coconut oil

Dash of salt

For the topping:
¼ cup toasted shredded coconut
¼ cup chopped pecans

Directions:

Place the sauce pan over medium-high heat and add butter, syrup, almond extract, cherry liqueur, coconut oil and salt. Cook until well melted and stir to blend.
Pour the mixture into a glass baking dish and refrigerate for 3 hours.
Pace the toppings in separate plates and start with preparation; cut the almond butter mixture into 15 slices and roll each slice with hands until you have a ball.
Roll each ball in toppings and set in paper cases.
Refrigerate until ready to serve.

Nutritional Info: Per serving

Calories: 103
Total fat: 11.2g

Cholesterol: 24mg
Total Carbs: 0.9g

Protein: 0.2g

*I*CY BNERRY DESSERT

Preparation Time: 10 minutes + inactive time   Servings: 4

*I*ngredients:

2 cups blackberries
1 cup heavy cream
1 tablespoons sugar-free syrup

2 cups ice, crushed
¼ cup fresh mint, chopped

*D*irections:

Place syrup, fruits, ice, heavy cream, and mint in food processor. Pule until well blended and pour into baking dish; refrigerate for 30 minutes. Scrape with fork and refrigerate for 1 hour. Spoon into glasses and serve. Serve with love.

*N*utritional *I*nfo: *P*er serving

Calories: 139   Cholesterol: 41mg   Protein:1.8g
Total fat: 11.5g   Total Carbs: 7.7g

*B*ANANA CHIA PUDDING

Preparation Time: 10 minutes + inactive time   Servings: 2

*I*ngredients:

1 ripe banana
4 tablespoons chia seeds
½ cup heavy cream

½ teaspoon vanilla
½ teaspoon cinnamon

*D*irections:

Place banana, vanilla, cream, and cinnamon in food processor.
Pulse until well combined and add chia seeds.
Pulse couple times to mix evenly.
Serve in dessert cups and refrigerate for 1 hour before serving.

*N*utritional *I*nfo: *P*er serving

Calories: 321   Cholesterol: 0mg   Protein: 4,8g
Total fat: 30.0g   Total Carbs: 14.5g

*B*AKED CHOCOLATE MOUSSE

Preparation Time: 10 minutes
Cooking time: 30 minutes
Servings: 6

*I*ngredients:

3 tablespoons pure cocoa
¼ cup water

3 Erythritol
2 oz. bitter sweet chocolate

0.5 oz. unsweetened chocolate
¼ teaspoon vanilla extract
½ tablespoon white rum
Dash of salt

1 cup heavy cream
1 egg + 1 egg white
Some fresh raspberries - to garnish

Directions:

Preheat oven to 350F and spray 8-inch spring form with cooking oil.

Bring water to boil in sauce pan over medium heat.

Stir in the cocoa and continue stirring until dissolves. Add chocolates and stir as well.

Transfer the mixture into a bowl and set aside; stir occasionally to avoid that crust that may form.

Make double boiler with pot of boiling water and oven proof bowl ate the top. Add the egg. Beat egg white and Erythritol in oven proof bow and whisk constantly for 2 minutes.

Remove the oven proof bowl from the heat, and using electric whisk, whisk the eggs until fluffy.

Fold the eggs into chocolate and stir gently until well mixed.

Add whipped cream and stir again, until well incorporated.

Transfer the mixture into prepared spring form and bake for 25-28 minutes.

Set on wire rack to cool, then transfer to the refrigerator and chill for 4 hours.

Slice before serving and serve with some fresh raspberries.

Nutritional Info: Per serving

Calories: 103
Total fat: 9.7g

Cholesterol: 55mg
Total Carbs: 2.9g

Protein: 2.7g

GINGER CRÈME BRULEE

Preparation Time: 10 minutes   Cooking time: 30 minutes   Servings: 6

Ingredients:

7 egg yolks
½ teaspoon vanilla extract
3 cups heavy coconut cream

1/3 cup Erythritol
1 teaspoon finely ground ginger

Directions:

Heat the oven to 350F.

Beat the egg yolks with erythritol and vanilla, until thick and creamy.

Transfer the cream into sauce pan, add ginger and heat over medium heat until it almost come to boil.

Stir the heavy cream into egg mixture and whisk until combined.

Now, pour the mixture into the top of double boiler. You can also drain it through sieve if you want to remove ginger pieces. Stir for 3 minutes and pour into shallow ceramic oven-proof dish.

Bake for 30 minutes in preheated oven and set on wire rack to cool.

Refrigerate for 1 hour.

Serve after.

Nutritional Info: Per serving

Calories: 341
Total fat: 33.9g

Cholesterol: 245mg
Total Carbs: 7.6g

Protein: 5.9g

CHESTNUT CREAM

Preparation Time: 10 minutes   Cooking time: 10 minutes   Servings: 6

Ingredients:

1.5 cup heavy cream
½ cup milk
1 can chestnut puree
½ cup can chopped pears

½ teaspoon vanilla extract
1 ½ teaspoon gelatin, unflavored + 2 tablespoons water
1 ½ tablespoon amaretto

Directions:

Combine water and gelatin in a small bowl.

Mix milk and cream into sauce pan, and heat over medium-high heat and bring to boiling point, but do not boil. Add some of the milk mixture to the gelatin, stir well and stir in the sauce pan with the milk and cream. Place the vanilla extract, amaretto and chestnut puree in food processor. Pulse until well blended and stir in the milk-cream mixture.

Divide between six molds or smaller bowls and refrigerate overnight.

To serve; dip the molds in hot water and flip onto plate.

Heat chopped pears, with juice in small sauce pan over medium-high heat.

Cook for couple minutes until you have slightly thick juice.

Pour over chestnut cream and serve.

Nutritional Info: Per serving

Calories: 138
Total fat: 11.5g

Cholesterol: 43mg
Total Carbs: 4,8g

Protein: 2.3g

KETO BROWNIES

Preparation Time: 10 minutes   Cooking time: 30 minutes   Servings: 12

Ingredients:

1 ½ cups butter
1 cup sugar-free syrup
1 egg
1 teaspoon vanilla extract

½ cup cacao powder
½ cup chocolate chips or carob chips, sugar-free
1 teaspoon baking soda

Directions:

Preheat oven to 350F and line a 9-inch baking pan with parchment paper.

In a large bowl whisk all ingredients together and stir in chocolate chips.

Transfer the batter into lined baking pan and smooth the surface with a silicone spatula.

Bake for 25-30 minutes until the brownies are done, but still soft in the middle.

Allow cooling before you slice it.

Nutritional Info: Per serving

Calories: 257
Total fat: 25.5g

Cholesterol: 76mg
Total Carbs: 6.9g

Protein: 2.2g

*I*CY COCONUT

Preparation Time: 10 minutes   Servings: 4

Ingredients:
1 cup coconut cream   4 tablespoons melted coconut oil
1 teaspoon vanilla extract   3 teaspoons cocoa powder
Few drops stevia

Directions:
Combine the coconut cream, vanilla, and stevia in a bowl. Pop in the freezer.
Pulse until smooth and refrigerate while you prepare the chocolate topping.
Melt coconut oil in microwave. Stir in cocoa powder.
Scoop the ice cream into small bowls and drizzle with chocolate topping.
Serve and enjoy.

Nutritional Info: Per serving
Calories: 261   Cholesterol: 0   Protein: 2.6g
Total fat: 28.1g   Total Carbs: 4.2g

*K*ETO BROWNIE PIE

Preparation Time: 10 minutes
Cooking time: 30 minutes
Servings: 6

Ingredients:
6 eggs   3 tablespoons coconut oil, melted
¾ cup unsweetened cocoa powder   2 teaspoons vanilla
¾ cup sugar-free syrup   Pinch of salt

Directions:
Preheat oven to 350F and lightly grease a pie pan with some coconut oil.
In a large bowl whisk eggs, coco powder, syrup, coconut oil, vanilla and salt.
Transfer batter into the prepared pie pan and smooth the top with a spatula.
Bake in the preheated oven for 30 minutes.
Place on a wire rack to cool before slicing and serving.
NOTE: You can dust cake with some cocoa powder before serving.

Nutritional Info: Per serving
Calories: 193   Cholesterol: 164mg   Protein: 9.3g
Total fat: 15.4g   Total Carbs: 11.3g

COOKIE DOUGH DIP

Preparation Time: 10 minutes

Servings: 4

Ingredients:

2 cups blanched almond flour
½ cup butter
¼ cup sugar-free syrup

1 tablespoon vanilla extract
½ teaspoon salt
½ cup chopped pecan nuts

Directions:

In a bowl combine almond flour, butter, syrup, vanilla and salt.
Fold in chopped pecan nuts.
Serve.

Nutritional Info: Per serving

Calories: 260
Total fat: 26.5g

Cholesterol: 61mg
Total Carbs: 3.9g

Protein: 2.7g

COOKIE DOUGH TRUFFLES

Preparation time: 15 minutes + chilling time

Servings: 10 truffles

Ingredients:

1/2 cup butter, softened
3/4 cup Erythritol
1 teaspoon vanilla
2-1/4 cups blanched almond flour
14 oz. heavy cream

¾ cup mini chocolate chips, no sugar addedd

To coat:
1 1/2 lb. chocolate disks or chocolate chips

Directions:

In large bowl cream butter and eyrthritol with electric mixer.
Add vanilla and mix until incorporated; add flour, gradually followed with milk. Mix until combined thoroughly.
Stir chocolate chips with wooden spoon.
Form 1-inch balls from the mixture and set on baking sheet lined with parchment paper.
Chill for 2 hours in refrigerator; melt chocolate chips in double boiler.
Dip cookie balls into melted chocolate, using two forks until completely covered.
Set on waxed paper and chill for 1 hour or until chocolate is firm.
Serve after.

Nutritional Info: Per serving

Calories: 303
Total fat: 29.0g

Cholesterol: 82mg
Total Carbs: 8.2g

Protein: 3.5g

PEANUT BUTTER COOKIE DOUGH TRUFFLES

Preparation time: 60 minutes   Servings: 70 truffles

Ingredients:

1.5 stick butter, softened
3/4 cup Erythritol
14oz. heavy cream
1 teaspoon vanilla
3/4 cup peanut butter
1/4 teaspoon salt

2 ¼ cups blanched almond flour
½ cup mini chocolate chips
1 pkg. vanilla coating, sugar-free
½ cup peanut butter chips
2 teaspoons shortening

Directions:

Cream butter and erythritol in large mixing bowl.

Add vanilla extract and peanut butter; mix to combine.

Gradually add condensed milk and mix until blended.

Stir in chocolate chips with spatula.

Form 1-inch balls from the mixture and set on baking sheet lined with parchment paper.

Set in freezer for 30 minutes.

Melt coating according to package Directions; place prepared balls in coating and stir until coated entirely.

Set balls onto waxed paper and in fridge until coating is firm.

Meanwhile, combine peanut butter chips and shortening in microwave safe bowl.

Set in microwave for 20 seconds on high; remove stir and continue process until completely melted and combined.

Remove balls from the freezer and drizzle with prepared peanut mix.

Set in freezer until firm and serve.

Nutritional Info: Per serving

Calories: 70
Total fat: 6.9g

Cholesterol: 15mg
Total Carbs: 1.8g

Protein: 2.0g

CONCLUSION

The Ketogenic diet is a type of diet that can offer so many positive health benefits in addition to weight loss. Unlike other types of diet, this diet is proven to work and according to medical studies this low-carb diet came out ahead in comparison to other diets. The Ketogenic diet is a healthy option to lose weight without having to fear for health and your wallet.

Ketogenic diet actually do not deserve word "diet" in name, it should be named as a chance for better and healthier life. With each bite of food prepared according to Keto rules we are investing in healthier future life, without extra pounds, high blood sugar levels and lower blood pressure – health issues of almost all of us

Once you get used to low-carb lifestyle, things tend to become easier and you are likely to see some impressive results which will ultimately lead to a healthier, slimmer and happier you.

Thank you again for purchasing this book!

Finally, if you enjoyed this book, please take the time to share your thoughts and post a review on Amazon. It'd be greatly appreciated!

Feel free to contact me at emma.katie@outlook.com

Check out more books by Emma Katie at:

www.amazon.com/author/emmakatie

CPSIA information can be obtained
at www.ICGtesting.com
Printed in the USA
BVHW010212021020
590162BV00013B/191